MW01166068

2023 New Generation Beats Anthology

New Generation Beats

National Beat Poetry Foundation, Inc.

Deborah Tosun Kilday - Pamela Twining

The National Beat Poetry Foundation, Inc. would like to dedicate this years anthology to the memory of Pamela Twining, State of New York Beat Poet Laureate. She was a passionate human being and exceptional poet. Her words were meaningful and she believed in living in a natural way, doing no harm to others or the environment, only showing love, caring and kindness to all. Her loss to the poetry community is great. She is an example of what it means to be a poet in the true sense of the word. I'm posting a photo from the 2022 Nat'l & Int'l Beat Poetry Festival where I had the great honor of presenting Pamela with this award, naming her State of New York Beat Poet Laureate. Her voice may have been silenced, but her words will live on forever.

You can find in our anthologies Pamela's words and see some of her past performances on our YouTube Channel. https://www.youtube.com/@nationalbeatpoetryfoundati5845/videos

Published by
New Generation Beat Publications

Copyright 2023
by
New Generation Beat Publications

All Rights Reserved

ISBN: 978-1-957654-08-9

Debbie Tosun Kilday - Editing & Cover Design.

Human Error Publishing - Editing & Formatting

TABLE OF CONTENTS

KIMBER ACRYLIC

"Haunted accent"

Slow dancing with emaciated cryptids denying their legends,
I feign superstition and luck.

Earth's haunted accent taunts the poppy scented
emasculate Armageddon that arrives effeminate.

Cocaine stained solstice melts and falters beneath the drunk,
organic path of famine.

Valium stars blow kisses from the traumatic vomiting sky
the rusted roof of the lands.

Cigarette burns on burial grounds of soft, mad poets chain-
smoking their grief with decay.

Whispering your lament with caffeine scented breath, eyes
sewn shut with tears, we're free!

Kimber Acrylic has been writing poetry for over 30 years.
Her contribution in the community is vast. Her work has been
in several anthologies alongside the likes of IAMX, Sadie
Frost, Michael Madsen, Charlie Sheen, even collaborating
post death with Andy Warhol. She is currently planning on
releasing her most recent volume of poetry.

DONNA ALLARD

sundial

today is a day to take a path less traveled, as Dryas seed-heads
and dragonflies welcome the dawn

just past the pines a weathered farm, generations of toil
you can also tell by the additions of rooms over time

old rose bush's wreath: no entry : the chimney is a sundial

i cleared the front porch bench to rest a bit, to the left overgrown
apple trees, to my right a path leading to the creek where old fallen
timbers allow me to cross the cold teal waters

a blue heron cautiously lands along a short grass path combed by
moose or deer. the sun is full now and the Jack pine shade is fading
as i found a branch to use as a walking stick

in the distance woodpeckers carving out trees for their hidden delicacies
all is right with the world
the sundial says noon

Donna Allard award winning author, Canada, resides down a long dirt road and lives in a 1909 homestead where muses fill her world with flowing visual poetry. In 2019 was awarded the International New Generation Beat Poet Laureate by the National Beat Poetry Foundation Inc. CT USA. Ms. Allard is also a member of the League of Poets, AAAPNB and Carfac.

MICHAEL D. AMITIN

"The Exquisite Relief of Alphonse"

February, lemmings scurry up powder mountain
snort blue air
dip fine wine firelight boogie
very-white shapely sloped alps
ski vacation it's called here

foggy town paris
the poor stick around, stocking
grocery store shelves, sweeping rue de funk
afterhour sip the slippery slopes of alley cheap booze

keep your powder dry
store king hollers
over zoom gloom
to the working crew

alphonse takes a horse-size piss
scratches his
daily double, lady luck
shines him a quarter moon
over three cent town -
takes another shot and says
fuck the alps

Michael D. Amitin - Poet and musician from the
American West moved to Paris, France in 2009.
Named International Beat Poet Laureate 2020-2021
Amitin's poems have been published in Poetry Pacific,
California Quarterly, LoveLove Magazine, North of
Oxford, and can be found on his FB or Instagram page.

C.C.ARSHAGRA

No one owns the wind

Dedicated to Jack Shea
Producer of the documentary "Who Owns Jack Kerouac."

No one owns the wind
And the sunsets roll over roads
And they only rise to be
Memories remain here now

Remembering ashes
Joining the full return of emptiness,
And the love of words unpossessed

C.C. Arshagra is primarily a poet. The author, of "the open microphone / human rights, free speech and the word / A 20th Anniversary Edition"
Arshagra's works in multiple mediums all culminate in one voice and that is to free the voices of all. Producer, publisher, lyric writer, lecturer, painter, free speech activist and concept creator.

DR. SANTOSH BAKAYA

The Stentor

I tick another day on the calendar,
and time spurs on. Galloping away.
Another today becomes yesterday.
I once again dream- New dreams
-dreams of winning a marathon race,
 crushing that malevolent smile
from the demagogue's face.

I dream,
not of experiencing the craziest river rapid
[That would be a nightmare!]
 or touching the highest mountain peak.
But I just sit and dream vacuous dreams,
 ticking days on the calendar, nonchalantly.
Twiddling thumbs, staring into nothingness.
Not bothered about the thought:
Who will clean the mess?
Did someone convince me
that ticking off days was a good pastime?

The Stentor spoke on, weaving lie after lie.
 "Fie on you! Fie!" Said that pesky little voice inside me.
[This yakitiyakking can be so nerve-wracking, you know!]

"Shake, shake, Wake- Wake.
Why are you so silent? Have you no tongue?"
"I am just a pipsqueak, what difference
will my speaking make to this bleak world?"

What will be the culmination of these
falsehoods and fulmination?
I yanked myself away from this rumination,
and once again started ticking days-
Days for the Stentor's comeuppance.

With a shudder, I realized that all along
I had kind of felt conveniently snug
being out of sync with reality.
And reality! It was far from snug!
Ghoulish silhouettes and eerie sounds were hounding me.
Irritating. Persistent.
Oh, there were more sounds; existential sounds.
Sunday morning sounds and smells.
The water running, the smell of burnt toast,
 refrigerator door slamming.
Cups, saucers, pans, and platters, clattering.
Flipping pancakes in the skillet needed focus.
Focus- Please Focus.
The worldly hocus – pocus could wait.
Justice and fairness could wait.

A cauldron bubbling- Bubbling- Bubbling.
Superimposing itself into these Sunday morning sounds,
 a Stentor speaking stridently. Unstopping.
Churning one falsehood after another.
And yet another.

Dr. Santosh Bakaya is a multiple award-winning writer,
poet, novelist, essayist, biographer, creative writing mentor,
and TEDx speaker. She has penned more than twenty-three
books across different genres, many of which have been
Amazon bestsellers. Her poetic biography of Mahatma
Gandhi, Ballad of Bapu, and Only in Darkness can you see
the Stars [Biography of Martin Luther King Jr.] have been
internationally acclaimed.

RANDY BARNES

The Media Scoops Its Loot

Bent language and altered meanings
no shortage of chatter matter
it's penis love for Heads of State
a built-in scenery with blemish erosion
terminal fly grab and shoulder lurch
pie in the sky to reset the soul
tripped up and ripped off
back-burner never-minds
a license for climax to open the stacks
channel slip on sky alert
layers loaded for purge
a low-brow revenge come to deliver.

Randy Barnes has published far and wide since the early
1970s. Many poems in Lit Mags and Anthologies with three
slim volumes of poems now long out of print. He was
 awarded a Lifetime Historian Beat Poet Laureate for
Washington State in 2020 from the National Beat Poetry
Foundation, Inc.

CARLOS BARRERA

"ALCHEMY"

Symbols of forbidden power
Dark brown eyes of an eternal gaze
Empty dawns & crimson twilights
Solitudes
And wasted days.

Life goes on & death's still waiting
Eager to consume the rhyme
Everything is temporary
But oblivion
Will be mine.

Couple virtues never chosen
Sins that tear apart my soul
Thousand miles I ain't ever traveled
From where diamonds turn
To coal.

And these hands were born for diggin'
Neath those Harlan County skies
Tryin' to find a better meaning
To them words
I alchemize.

Symbols
These are merely symbols
Lines that will erase the tide
Alibis to carry with you
In a long & endless ride.

Carlos Barrera's poetry is mostly influenced by the Spanish
Generations of '98 & '27 & the American Beat Generation.
As a bilingual writer his work's been published in several
independent magazines in Spanish as "Vents d'Ahir" &
"Nueva poesía andaluza" & in English in some recent
anthologies by the National Beat Poetry Foundation.
Actually lives in Mexico City.

Eşref OZAN BAYGIN

THE BASTARD'S YEAR (II)

Between delusion and reality
Closer to the truth
With the effect of the first fallen word
I fell asleep and
Then spiders guarded my cave.

I waited for my slap
That makes no secret of his voice
With the prophets, -without midwives
The bat cubs gnawing on my left ear,
The left ear buzzing and the rising decibel of whispers are
sacred psychosis.

THE BASTARD'S YEAR (III)

By the action of alkaloids gushing from hidden organs
suddenly the deluge
as fast as the waves
spread to the beaches
at a speed of 1,500 kilometers per hour

The tramp who witnessed the discoloration of his tarpaulin is
inside the balcony
He wanted to sit in the clouds with the power of thought and
Buildings began to stand in homage

Poets who laugh almost to overthrow,
a boundless void into which is fallen
by fake smiles that don't own any passion
and a long trip heads to the parallel universe,

shivering in parks and empty benches, his jaw locked
the tomb that destroys time,

the butterfly which flutters around the candle,
"bong roulette" in "Tesadüf"
At the level of the most sacred friendship,
At 06:30 in the morning, passengers listening to bubbles,
holy generation
to defend their craziness to live free and,
they are doomed to hide their craziness in order to live free.

The last deer to jump on the ice
the last worm out of the black hole
the last shapeless melting piece of ice
Huxley's holy island and the secret
We have to pull the last smoke hard
or else how do we know this holy truth?

Okay, let's move
let's go to the womb of the sky
this is what the wise Einstein wanted.
the smile of the stars drives us crazy.

Ozan Baygın (Eşref Ozan Baygın)(Eţref Ozan Baygýn)
was born in 1993 in Istanbul. He is still studying and writing
on high level education in Yıldız Tecnical University. His
poems have been published in anthologies and magazines
in many different countries. In total he has published six
books. In addition to this literary work, he has released three
music albums. His works include "LSD OR COINCIDENCE,"
"PSYCHEDELIC POETRY" (Yazarkafa Magazine, no.20),
and "Beat Generation" (Yazarkafa Magazine, no. 22).

ERIC BELMER

Character Defamation

I revel in dramatic appearances and
I die for the acting
I appreciate the incendiary flare
...Until it becomes real
Taken as gossip
Taken out of context.
Before it becomes a blade
Housing teenage-based nightmares.
Emotions rampant and accosted.
Words unfiltered and directed.
For the stab wounds
That litter my back.
The drama represented
With seething tranquility for one
And only one.
That's not drama
Call her manipulation and malevolence.
Whom did you speak to
That filled your callous mouth
With only negativity?
Words have power darling.
I've erred and stared at our faults
A species dance.
Where communication loses light,
And becomes an after thought.
Where words become weapons,
Tools to draw the masses.
Get your pitchforks
The monster has entered the act.
Smile bright
Lights! Camera! Action!
I'm your creature horror delight.

Erik Belmer is a poet based out of Portland Maine. He is a professional bartender that loves inventing cocktails when he isn't using his creativity for poetry. He is very active in the spoken word scene in Portland ME and Portsmouth NH. The themes of his work stem from love, heartbreak, self-image and existential ponderings. He has two books out Cupid's Carrying A 45 and Perfecting The Act Of Drowning.

BENGT O BJÖRKLUND

relentless in motion

dire in intent
self appointed lawmen
rule the after hours
with whips and threats
of stolen exposures

billboards praise you
whispers of a dying planet
pleases you and I rules
of safeguarding wealth
still counts for more than death
even ants or slugs
must have a vote a say
at the end of all goodbyes

****

I see doubters in the sky
worried faces rolling
running for office
in countries where flags
burst into fire on any given day
ruled by the unfair and the dead

selected and unruled
we the few with scars and tissue
crawl in the solitude of I
for the sake of no war
no killing no hate
we also reject indifference

steeped in still back water
weary men run for cover
as tactile bombs
fall from skinny enemy skies
where dark rabbits
do worry about the end of time

streamed and crying
I see your need to grasp
and understand
the dervish madness
the spitting image of a life
in an oyster's dream

I see the dull I see shaved
buddhist calamity on fire
with nothing to say
breathing heavily
in white man's privilege soup
bowing just for the sake of it

time is a walk to the cinema
while the posters are printed
a dive into the pool
before the unfurnished
leave their red mark
on the new born baby

sometimes between here
and the logs not yet ignited
I dream of soya cream
whipped into days gone
I will not yield or pray
this is just another day

pious men's relief
in dark slaughterhouses
run by a religion
where animals bleed
is all for the sake
of being more than one

****

ruled by the fire of the night
stored in the afterbirth of all
that descends into the here
where no solitude

can relive the testimonies
of silent extinction
dead men sellin dead flowers
at the market of one man
going to war
with nothing but pathology
dressed up for surgery

so that night I met
your mother all done up
in scorched finery
and a disposition towards scorn
solemnity and weather
ran for a seat
in the local portrait
of Dorian Gray
various factions of stuntmen
found their addresses
sold to the highest bidder

Bengt O Björklund - Lifetime Beat Poet Laureate was born in Stockholm, Sweden 1949. Since the mid seventies he has eleven published poetry collections in Swedish and English.

CHRIS BODOR

This Place

It is amazing how
You can change a life with one word
That goes for bad words
That goes for good words.

When I close the window and lock my door
I no longer surround myself with you,
I no longer know you, and sadly, and suddenly
I remove myself from what makes this place a "place".

Goodbye land of sand.
Goodbye salt water.
Goodbye sunshine.

This town can be a diseased piece of meat
Spewing warped words when they mistakenly meet
One day, this town will meet the maker
One day, they will bump into each other in the elevator.

I am erasing the footage
Of the documentary film of my adolescence.
Fear is a foamy film, I can punch through it
Fear is a foamy film, I can walk through it.

Hello land of sand.
Hello salt water.
Hello sunshine.

Chris Bodor is a first generation American, born in CT to an English mother and a Hungarian father. During the past three decades, his poems have appeared in many independent, small, and micro-press publications, such as the Lummox Journal, Live Nude Poems, and New Generation Beats-2022 Anthology. Bodor is the Editor-In-Chief of the international literary journal A.C. PAPA, which stands for Ancient City Poets, Authors, Photographers, and Artists.

JULIE BOLT

Flow

I am the mother, the witch, the huntress, the sage,
the mystic, the lover
I am the lover, the mystic, the gatherer, the pagan,
the daughter, the waif
I am the waif, the traveler, the healer, the explorer,
the community worker
I am the worker, the soother, the disruptor, the raven,
the wolf and the spider
I am the spider, the weaver, the worker, the lover, the sister,
the peasant, the sorcerer
I am the sorcerer, the child, the crone, the disruptor,
the crazy, the fortress, the leader
I am the leader, the needer, the sister, the misfit, the
potential, the gift and the power
I am the power, the listener, the friend, the embracer,
the giver, the taker
I sit by your side, link eyes, move with movement

I'm water

Julie Bolt is an educator, poet, essayist and intersectional
advocate. She's grew up in Greenwich Village, NYC and
then lived and traveled widely. Now she is a tenured
Associate Professor of English at Bronx Community College.
Her poetry, flash and essays have appeared in print and
online journals and anthologies, Her first collection of poetry
is Time Sensitive and her book on decolonial education is
Border Pedagogy for Democratic Practice.

MATTHEW BOWERS

Beat Child

Beat Child, Beat Child
Running wild
Through the streets
Raw Emotion
Full of heat
Pounding to the beat
Against the wall
Standing tall
I'll follow her
To the end of time

Slippery wet
Silhouette
Your name and number
Tattooed on my mind
Lest I forget this moment in time
I believe

Pin Eyed girl
Porcelain skin
I never knew
Whose dream I was in
Clara Bow style
Double agent smile
I always looked both ways
Before I crossed
That street

Maybe you don't remember
I know I'll never forget
The dancing, the cocktails
The darkness... regret

The sun always burned
In the night
We came to life
You punctured my heart

Like a switchblade knife

Beat Child, Beat Child
Running wild
I'll follow her
To the end of time

Matthew Bowers is a LA based published author, writer, poet, and artist. He has featured with Ron Whitehead on The New Beat Generation Manifesto. His latest writings appear in several NBPF©, New Generation Beat Publications anthologies.

R. BREMNER

Jazzed faces

Jazzed faces
Weary psyches
Smells of coffee and
Pre-dawn America
Sallow moon
Waiting for us

Snake eyes
Dog breath
Here in a night
Of pals and gals
In this cannabis home

On the beach
Laying surreptitiously
With silicon dreams
Silicon hopes
For a new day
Of perfect lust
Perfect love

Breast of fortune
Womb divine
Brain of wonder
Woman, thou art
God's gift to man

Quick snatched phrases
From mouths of poets
Walking to and fro
On streets of Passaic
Where we all live
And sometimes die

Howls of thunder
Howls of laughter
And Ginsberg tears

Wrapped in a neat bundle
Amid fears and whispers
Under the Christmas tree

Sunlight screaming
anodynes streaming
filling the void
inside our minds
with capsicum and Buddha

screaming sunlight
actionable moonlight
soothe our fears
as escaping sounds
eat our ears

R. Bremner has spent a wasted and useless life. his putrid work has soiled the pages of International Poetry Review, Quarterday, Passaic Review issue #1 with Allen Ginsberg, Anthem: a Leonard Cohen Tribute, Climate of Opinion: Sigmund Freud in Poetry, etc. he has published eight print books (Cajun Mutt Press), and has thrice won honors in the Allen Ginsberg Awards. ron lives with his beautiful sociologist wife of 34 years in wonderful Northeast New Jersey.

SHEILA LOWE-BURKE/ SHEILA BURKE

Summer of '69

In the Summer of '69

We looked for love

Drank the wine

Prayed for peace

Marched in the street

Shed our clothes

Looked for those

Who found the answers

Blowin' in the wind

Then did it again.

In my Summer of 69

I've found the love

Savored the wine

Sung for peace

Marched in the streets

Cast off the cloak

Of hypocrisy

Found the answers

Hidden within

And I'd do it all

Again and again.

10/23/2022

Sheila Lowe-Burke, aka Sheila Burke -A warded an honorary doctorate for her life work in peace and social justice, born in eastern Ky. Attended University of Pikeville, studied liberal arts and theology. Completed business degree, Spring Arbor University. A single mom, business consultant, and vocal soloist. Presently touring and performing with music and life partner Joe Kidd, writing, recording, and producing poetry, lyrics, illustrated grand-mother story poems and children's literature.

JOHN BURROUGHS

Bearing Her

She's in sunny Somewhere driving
while I'm in rainy Right Here drinking
Awestruck Lovestruck cider and a couple
of IPAs, listening to November Rain in
March at Water Street Brewery, thinking
it's her street in an obfuscated state
as I see her in my pint glass and on
the server's Hellcat shirt and lingering near
the liquor shelves, and in every other
corner of the jukebox and my world
is awash in her being and bearing.

John Burroughs of Cleveland is U.S. Beat Poet Laureate
(2022-2023) and previously served for two years as Ohio's
Beat Poet Laureate. He is the author of Rattle & Numb:
Selected and New Poems, 1992-2019 [2019, Venetian
Spider], You Can't Trust It to Remain [2022, Between
Shadows], Dogging Catastrophe [2022, The Grind Stone]
and more than a dozen earlier collections. Since 2008, John
has served as the founding editor of Crisis Chronicles Press.
You may find him at crisischronicles.com.

DOUGLAS G. CALA

Clash of Titans

Poet as prophet
Poet as philosopher
Poet as ideological disperser
Poet as pedagogue
Poetry as lifeblood
Poets as resistance fighters
Poets as activists
Poets as revolutionaries
Poets as being held responsible for new ages

Berserker rage blooms,
Like gladiators in a tireless sphere fight
swinging archaic but powerful weaponry
Berserker rage blooms,
Battle scars worn by everyone,
Testaments of survival,
Everywhere and nowhere simultaneously
Mighty men fall every day,
Susceptible to poisonous logic that's damning civilization
Warbirds, tactical drones, not the answer
Laying waste to innocence, civilian casualty on the uptick
For pointedly precise power plays pack punches
Fates decided with the immediacy of a swift gavel
Lock him away! Lock him away!
Strait jackets are not enough to contain turbulent minds,
As one-sided adjudicators think mental illness mythical,
Fare-beaters jump turnstiles with reckless abandon,
Inflation prices suffocate impoverished,
Derelicts misplaced in a broken system,
Citywide mayors' crackdown!
For berserker rage still blooms
In communities
In nations, as kids witness their parents flayed,
Strife predating their lifetimes, trivialities enmeshing
Muted therapy sessions
Solidification of axioms
Bandages come off, now no wounds

Douglas G. Cala is a spoken word performance poet and photographer/videographer from New York. He got his start on the café open mic circuit in the mid-2000s and has gone on to headline many predominantly East Coast performance venues with feature showcases. He has been published in a variety of zines, magazines, and anthologies. He can be found in the Poets & Writers directory as a Spoken Word Artist at Douglas G. Cala | Directory of Writers from Poets & Writers (pw.org).

DON KINGFISHER CAMPBELL

The Latest Headlines

Flies decide to start washing feelers
to eliminate diseases picked up from
roadkill.

Hermaphrodite sea cucumbers declare
themselves a disgrace to the planet.

Fish will no longer allow sex changes
to save species--goodbye cruel world!

Mice experiment on larger life forms
to promote tolerance.

Frogs plan to stop licking own skin
to get high.

Bird songs copyrighted to prevent
those not of their kind from
using their mating rituals.

Rabbits vow to become monogamous
--must control their soap opera lives
to curtail nose and tail twitching.

Cats and dogs unite to put an end
to unwanted pregnancies,
bite each other's balls off.

Hyenas quell laughter--Earth
just isn't funny anymore.

Monkeys, in an effort to advance
their lot on the globe, promise
to limit acts of masturbation
and oral sex to once a month.

Lions abolish war against gazelles
--remarkable weight loss and
reduction in heart attacks reported
--grass tastes good!

Pandas proclaim there is only one God
--and it is in their own image.

Dolphins can dancing from
their swim routines--there's
too much art on this sphere.

Zebras paint themselves completely
black or white in an attempt
to head off horse prejudice.

Humans still displaying animal
characteristics when it comes to
territoriality, homophobia, and drug abuse.

Elephants remember when looks
did not matter.

Whales release double CD of ocean tunes,
believe they're as talented as Yes.

Trees sway to celebrate a billion years
of being hooked on sunlight.

Clouds know they're above it all.

Don Kingfisher Campbell, MFA from Antioch University
L.A., taught at Occidental College Upward Bound for 36
years, been poetry editor of the Angel City Review, publisher
of Spectrum magazine, and host of the Saturday Afternoon
Poetry reading and workshop series in Pasadena, California.
For awards, features, and publication credits, please go to:
http://dkc1031.blogspot.com

VANESSA CARAVEO

The Haven Within Me

A safe and brave space I have found
to share my talents with the world
without worrying of feeling judged
or ridiculed for my unique thoughts and ideas.
Gone are the days I was the slave of
each negative comment which hurt my soul
like a dove with an injured wing who is
unable to fly to the heights it was destined for.

Now I fly without fear and full of confidence
for I have found this beautiful haven
where other have also had the valiance
to spread their wings and become messengers
sharing their voice and making a difference
in this chaotic yet beautiful world we live in.

With time, the long and challenging journey showed me
that safe and brave haven was inside of me all along
and now I inspire to help others find that haven
within themselves knowing this will enable us to reach
our highest self and prosper in life as we were meant to.

Vanessa Caraveo is an award-winning author, published poet, and artist whose literary work brings focus to various social issues that exist today. She has been published in Literature Today Journal, The Poet Magazine, Latinidad Magazine, Poetrybay, Anacua Literary Arts Review, and in multiple anthologies throughout the years.

MICHAEL CERAOLO

Theory, Not Practice

Trust the science
intone those in ignorance or disregard
of the second-grade science that says
dark colors absorb sunlight, making things hotter,
whereas light colors reflect sunlight,
keeping things cooler

Michael Ceraolo is a 65-year-old retired firefighter/
paramedic and active poet who has had two full-length
books (Euclid Creek, from Deep Cleveland Press; 500
Cleveland Haiku, from Writing Knights Press) published, and
has two more in the publication pipeline."

RICK CHRISTIANSEN

BONE FRAGMENTS
An archeological excavation

My mother would disappear, sometimes for up to a week.
I would shoplift groceries at the Ralph's in North Hollywood to
feed myblittle brother and myself. It didn't feel like stealing. I
always took a list.

I don't remember the movie by name. I was 8 or 9. I fell
hopelessly inblove with the beautiful princess. For the next
50 years, I was sure that I would find her in the bright eyes of
every neurotic narcissist I dated. I was always disappointed.
But she was always there.

I hate to carry a lot of change in my pockets. It reminds me
of when I had to go to the laundromat with my little brother. I
always tried to use some of the change to buy him candy. He
was easier to handle in public spaces when he had candy.

I was always reluctant to make promises to my children.
I didn't want to disappoint them.
I would just say "we'll see…"
when they asked for a commitment.
They were always disappointed.

I killed my dog yesterday. She was failing.
I killed her before she failed. I will never know
when she would have actually failed. I didn't wait
for the end of that movie.

I have built a life around listening to the music others make
and trying to match the syncopation. There is some peace
in slowly going deaf.
It isn't really silence,
just the absence of noise.

More artifacts-another layer:

My grandson told me that he thought going to prison would
be really "awesome"—
He said that it would be relaxing
to be forced into compliance.
Or basically that…

I got $10 an hour to model nude
for the art school in the 1970's.
I told my friends I was doing it for the money.
I was lying.

I tried to become an alcoholic
during my Freshman year of college.
I drank two warm beers for breakfast every day. But
then I went to class.
          I fucked it up.
I should have skipped class.

Last night I dreamed that I shaved off my beard.
My girlfriend broke up with me. Then I woke up.
I told her about the dream and she laughed…
"Yeah, how dare you change your appearance without my
permission!"

My biological mother was 17 when she conceived me.
My daughter was 17 when she conceived my grandson.
My grandson is now 17.
He lives with me.
I think about what he may be conceiving as I write this.

I lived with my great grandparents
          until I was three.
          Until my great grandfather
started having seizures.

I asked if he was going to get better.
If I was going to be able to come back
home to them.
They did not want to disappoint me.

They said "we'll see…"

Rick Christiansen is a former corporate executive, stand-up comedian, actor and director. His work is published or forthcoming in MacQueen's Quinterly, Oddball Magazine, Muddy River Poetry Review, Stone Poetry Journal, The Raven's Perch, The Rye Whiskey Review, As It Ought to Be Magazine, WINK Magazine and other journals, magazines and anthologies. He is the co-host of SpoFest and a member of The St. Louis Writers Guild. He lives in Missouri near his eight grandchildren.

PHILLIP HENRY CHRISTOPHER

I Know Neruda
(In Spanish- Yo Sé de Neruda)

I Know Neruda

I met a man
who said he knew
Neruda.
Soy de Chile.
I know
Neruda.

What about Allende?
I asked.

¿Quién?

He knew nothing
of Neruda.

I met a poet
who said he knew
Neruda.
Magical realism.
I know
Neruda.

What of love?
I asked.

What?

He knew nothing
of
Neruda.

I met a politician
who said he knew
Neruda.

Comunist.
I know
Neruda.

¡Ah, si!
Sube a nacer
conmigo, hermano.
¿Que?

¡Ah!
Dadme el silencio,
el agua, la esperanza.

¿Que?

He knew nothing
of
Neruda.

I met a child
who said he knew
Neruda,
played with
Neftalí
in
Temuco.

He knew everything
of
Neruda.

Yo Sé de Neruda
 (In Spanish)

Encontré a un hombre
que dijo sabía
de Neruda.

Soy de Chile.
Yo sé
de Neruda.

46

Pregunté,
¿Qué hay de Allende?

¿Quién?

No sabía nada
de Neruda.

Encontré a un poeta
que dijo sabía
de Neruda.

Realismo mágico.
Yo sé
de Neruda.

Pregunté,
¿Qué de amor?

¿Qué?

No sabía nada
de Neruda.

Encontré a un político
que dijo sabía
de Neruda.

Comunista.
Yo sé
de Neruda.

¡Ah, si!
Sube a nacer
conmigo, hermano.
¿Qué?

¡Ah!
Dadme el silencio,
el agua, la esperanza.

¿Qué?

No sabía nada
de Neruda.

Encontré un niño
que dijo que conocío
a Neruda,
jugó con
Neftalí
en
Temuco.

El sabía todo
de Neruda.

Phillip Henry Christopher was born In 1954 to a Greek
mother and American father of convoluted pedigree. Six
years later he began writing, and has been trying to figure it
out ever since. His poems and stories appear in print from
time to time, and his songs are often heard live or recorded
with various musicians in the loosely coordinated ensemble,
Peddler's French. While Phillip Henry Christopher writes the
songs, Philadelphia Phil sings and plays them.

ZOË CHRISTOPHER

Buddhist Clown School

Nothing funny about sitting on this zafu, eyes lowered like a
shackled concubine counting each breath, feeling only the
rise and fall of a shallow heartbeat, the weight of austerities,
teenage angst on the brink of screaming or dying.

We came here to practice breaking open, to learn to suffer
with dignity, to sacrifice the ordinary, to feed hungry ghosts
the sacred handbook for living in disguise.

Face to face with the Incredible Exploding Self, I learn to
giggle in silence: mom sleeping with the roshi, her husband
clueless and begging for enlightenment and praise.

Zoë Christopher is a poet and writer who has worn many
hats: ice-cream truck driver, waitress, addictions counselor,
astrologer, art installer, bookstore owner, photography
mentor, and program officer for a radical women's health
nonprofit, to name a few. She holds a Masters in
psychology and spent 20+ years providing supportive
intervention to various forms of adolescent and adult crises.
She's currently working on her memoir.

ANDY CLAUSEN

YOU IN THE PRIME OF LIFE

You in the prime of love with the future
You in the prime of life
You newer generations have the science to study
      many generations and you discovered
        how to use algorithms, cyber space, DNA
Those are big you can know so much
You've globalized knowledge
              made data instant
 But you also have made
              many disastrous mistakes
Judging the Gen I come from on your relationship
    & Interpretation of morality rejecting
      our past without context is one

I am of a different era
In Youth we were much happier than you all
Much more in love with expectations

And you would denigrate "cancel" and bury the art
             & literature of the past
     the previous generations generated
And every Artist will be looking over
           her or his shoulder
And all that will be available will be gutless work
           that never offends anyone
n a warm bath in my mind mitigating
      the pain & discomfort while writing
Like Marat did in the tub
       and does it mean Charlotte Corday
         will make her appearance?
Can I be like Adolph Fischer unjustly accused
      & convicted Hay Market Chicago protester
Eighteen nineties
Seconds before head snap on the noose
Shouting out on the gallows
"This is the happiest moment of my life."

My advancing age has emancipated my grey blues
           of guilt & pain, my intrepid honesty: I am free
Come and get me, yess, for I am accusing thee
           of trying to destroy all that is decent
                    & loving
I am accusing you of murdering Adolph Fischer
Accusing you of trying to vanquish all possible
           paths to   ah Justice--you better come
                    and get me

!The radical fellaheen prole peasant
           working hero dies
Eugene Everhard is gone
                    the heart is smashed!
The revolt crushed frightened into accepting
           a short budgeted existence as chattel
           as two-legged cattle
Experts of theological trickery present
           the gods & the God as adhesive
                    of civil society
The dark early days of November & December
           after the clocks got turned back

Years ago I often wrote standing up
I'd use a fireplace mantel hold my notebook
Twixt put to paper lines I danced
           about the room to instrumental music
Like right now this Dolphy
           Out There on Youtube

Truth now often I'm supine in bed
I used to compose linguistic snapshots
           in the Wild
A tree stump for a desk even for a lectern
I built a stone patio with flower box bench
           wrote both idylls and manifestos
I was Pericles pleading for Aspasia's Life
I was Bryan espousing the case of the ones
           working the land
I was old Common Sense at Valley Forge
I was, while Ollie our cat chased away

legions of tory horse flies
disruptive birds & growling squirrels

Andy Clausen is a former NY State Beat Laureate and is now a Lifetime Beat Poet Laureate. Allen Ginsberg said Andy was the best candidate to keep the Beat Generation alive and generating. He wrote, "Clausen inherited Neal Cassady's American Energy Transmission." He's the author of several books, most recently "BEAT: The Latter Days of the Beat Generation" and poetry books "40th Century Man", "Home of The Blues" and the soon to be released "THE FABLED DAMNED".

CLAIRE CONROY

Beat Sestina for a Stone

Dreamland boardwalk dock sidewalk chalk along the sea
Carefree squeal in sunshine briny wrinkled
fingers in the sand
Tanned and freckled through lotion lone Coppertone child
Wild ocean wind blown feathery flown girl seeking a rock
Requires to be shown desires earth bone unknown
mere stone
Touch hold steal aspire a thought or notion to feel

Dreamland boardwalk dock sidewalk reach the beach to feel
Wonder of the swirling potion churning roaring
emotion of sea
Tanned and freckled on the edge of this shore
gripping a stone
Flat and long ideal for skipping found on
the ground in the sand
Aspire flight hand whipping soaring dripping airborne rock
Slipping through lonely beguiled fingers
of the Coppertone child

Dreamland boardwalk dock sidewalk smiles
a plea at the wild child
Play more explore command the albacore to kneel and feel
Dipping waves reveal hiding in seaweed debris the rock
Among softened glass mild sea shells exiled from the sea
Within the enchanted zone where water kisses sand
The tanned little hand reached to the beach for the stone

Dreamland boardwalk dock sidewalk gawks
at the smooth stone
Along with the tanned and freckled Coppertone child
Dipping the pebble into the ocean to rinse the sand
Worn aged surface expired motion gives the gift of feel
An offering demands attentions from the throne of the sea
Shine of stone bone of earth pebble of promise a rock

Dreamland boardwalk dock sidewalk rejoices for the rock
The one those happy hands chose for one's own stone
Pocketed and loved throughout a day at the sea
By this wild tanned and freckled Coppertone child
Admired in the sun's gaze adored for the feel
Wishes rubbed in secret and abandon in the sand

Dreamland boardwalk dock sidewalk frames
these scenes in sand
Where our sunblocked moments can be kept with a lonely
rock
And a peanut butter and jelly sandwich kind of feel
Can be held in your salt stained memories like a stone
Where a pebble was placed by a Coppertone child
In a collection away from it's mothering sea

The pebble would never again see or feel the sand
But the sea saw this favorite day of this rock
And for 1,000 years the stone thanked the Coppertone child

Claire Conroy has a deep affection for words and their effects on readers. She has self published two books of poems ("Listen" 2018 and "Silent" 2022) and has also been published in global anthologies. You might find her at a coffee shop twisting words around while high on caffeine.

PW COVINGTON

I Live in the House that Jack Built

I live in the house that Jack built
I dine at a moveable feast
Through pastures of plenty on a Northbound train
A toast to 1969 and Flamingo Bar
Raising margarita glasses in Florida desolation

I live in the house that Jack built
I dine at a moveable feast
Accents in French
Or Spanish or hitchhike highway
Schizophrenia-driven Colorado madman
Preaching at a midnight North Beach bus stop

I live in the house that Jack built
I dine at a moveable feast
Mardi Gras mornings with beignets and chicory
Hired onto a Yugoslav freighter to Cork
Fleeing across the water
Staying ahead of gun smoke and seizures

I live in the house that Jack built
I dine at a moveable feast
The town and the city, ever behind me
Before me, a time-warp chimera
Sworn secret in that Salt Lake mirror-room
I am drinking hot drink, all the same

I live in the house that Jack built
I dine at a moveable feast
Discothèque Juarez checkpoint shakedowns
And years in Texas prison camps, be damned
Charleston motel meth market parking lot
Holding out hope for the next time at hand

I live in the house that Jack built
I dine at a moveable feast

In light-rail cars and hotel bars, I've seen them
Married to their misery, heaters set, 451 or more
Discount Southern states and churches
Flying Baptist values at the courthouse

I live in the house that Jack built
I dine at a moveable feast
Union busted freight car railroad sidings
In Laramie,
absconded with the last of last year's consequence
The clock keeps time for no one to take notice of
Retreating to secret libraries of eons

I live in the house that Jack built
I dine at a moveable feast
Catholic seminary run-away student
Circus clown and housewives
Theater ticket counter clerks and nurses
Writing it all down, for later
Later
Later

I live in the house that Jack built
I dine at a moveable feast

PW Covington writes in the Beat tradition of the North
American highway. He performs his work coast to coast, and
occasionally beyond. His work has been nominated for both
Pushcart and Best of the Net awards. In 2019, his North
Beach and Other Stories, was named an LGBTQ+ Fiction
Finalist by the International Book Awards. Covington lives
two blocks off Historic Route 66, in Northern New Mexico.

MIKAYLA CYR

"Sinister Seduction"

Stumbling through the dark
Chasing the echoes of your
tongue and cheek one liners
Tripping me into an ill-fated tomb
When did your heart become
the emptiest of rooms
Or has it always been this cold
This calloused
Spinning daydreams out of
lust and misintended malice
My mind says "no" while my soul
clings to whatever it can grab
Downing me in gulps whenever
it's convenient to have
A taste of sin, but only on your time
And darling, you've forgotten
I'm the tequila
Not the lime

Mikayla Cyr is a 29 year old Portland, ME native. A collector
of musical paraphernalia and tattoos, she finds herself
inspired by nature, love, loss, grief, and growth. She wrote
her first poem twenty-one years ago and hasn't stopped
since.

RODERICK DEACEY

PATIENCE IS A VIRTUE

So, small granddaughter,
this morning we are not learning about
birds, or trees, or flowers, or the weather.
Instead, we are going to talk about waiting—
which is why we are making our way
to the wooden bench at the railway station,
where we can contemplate the empty platforms,
listen to the bees buzzing about
in the Black-Eyed Susans
and wait.

Waiting is an essential learned skill—
there will never be any time in your life
when you are not waiting
for something or somebody.
We'll start with some easy examples:

waiting for the swimming pool to open
waiting for your mother to come collect you
waiting for your birthday to finally arrive
waiting to be old enough to go to school
waiting to be old enough to leave school
waiting to be old enough to leave home
waiting to be old enough to know better
waiting to catch that elusive fluttering bug of love
waiting for your prince to come
waiting for your prince to come home
waiting for your prince to come home from the war
waiting for the war to be over
waiting for your ship to come in
waiting for the other shoe to drop
waiting for the penny to drop
waiting to have your own children
waiting for payback, that bitch
waiting for your children to leave at last
waiting for your parents to leave at last
waiting to be free at last, free at last, thank God almighty…

waiting for freedom to be more than just some people talking
waiting for freedom to be a little less lonely
waiting for Godot—or Jesus
waiting for the rising tide to float your boat
waiting to live a little, then a little more
waiting to sing "Je ne regrette rien"
waiting to be content with "now" not "when"
waiting to be too old to worry about the world
waiting to replay those best memories
waiting for that to be almost enough
waiting for the rough beast, slouching
waiting for the last dance, a final pirouette
waiting to sleep, perchance…

We'll discuss all these things
when we are sitting at the station—
and how some things are worth the wait,
while other things aren't worth a damn!
Or we could, of course,
wait—
until you are somewhat older.

Anyway, the station is a good place
to learn about waiting—did you know
they even have a special room for it?
And, if we can simply wait for a while—
a heartbeat, a breath or two, a lifetime—
the train will come.

Roderick Deacey is a performing Beat poet, reading with
bass-player and drummer. He was awarded the 2019
Frederick Arts Council Carl R. Butler Award for Literature.
Crossing genres, he won the Gold Award for Best Lyrics in
the 2020 Mid-Atlantic Song Contest, plus the Silver Award
for Best Lyrics in 2022. His contemporary poems appear
regularly in literary journals.

WILLIAM F. DEVAULT

resurrect

laying down a beating where I'd been eating crow.
the blows are soft flesh on shattered sapphire.
too many business cards from timid MFAs,
mediocrities polluting Apollonian
streams of consciousness.
I am sorry that your husband died.
I acknowledge that you loved him,
and he, you, and I am grateful you found joy
to your own side of the Pillars of Heracles.
the fates did not hate us
but allowed us to stumble in blind bindings
until we crumbled
under the weight of our best pretensions.
cornbread corners to the hollow plates of desire.
I was unaware of the demon I found and bound
only with your persistent assistance. born of dragons
and chained in cinnabar and pitchblende.
pitchfork tongue
and the dung of desecration, left in the garden.
he calls for you from within his cell, where I starve him
with distractions and abstractions
while awaiting the resurrection
in a reinvented
winter that comes for us all
calling us liars as the fires fade
and we are paid up beyond the end of the stay
we had envisioned when we bought the condoms.
the halls and walls are as I envisioned them
described in the romantique's whispers
using words unheard in the most ancient places
where the Greek girl said I would find redemption.
she was wrong, but drunk at the time,
and I do not lay with the mysteries of Dionysius.
fire fire fire
inspire desire conspire with the smaller mind
blinded by a scent of honeysuckle
and night blooming jasmine.

reeling at the feeling of a greater death,
of self, beyond logic
and the toxic remembrances
that are mangled and tangled.
I gave up science and the truth of numbers
when I found that I would be always bound
by lesser minds, finding no freedom to discover
to uncover the essence of this transient life.

Previously appearing in TACHYON,
2020, Venetian Spider Press, ISBN: 978-1-7349469-2-5

William F. DeVault has over 30,000 poetic works in his primary catalog, and published more 30 volumes of these works, ranging from haiku to the volume liaison, which features 225 sonnets built as 15 heroic crowns. He is an NBPF US National Beat Poet Laureate Emeritus and was named by Yahoo "The Romantic Poet of the Internet".

CARLOS RAÚL DUFFLAR

Poetry for the People

I used to face the morning Sun
that lifted in the distance up the horizon of Alamo Park
the trees would fill the sky and surface
on this time of the morning
sitting by the kitchen table
and enjoying oatmeal, a cafecito and mango juice
in this place begins a new day
as Zahra will speak on current events
for filling the light of the world
it was time now to leave
and catch the bus beside the corner of Haight Street
so I kissed her and lifted a beautiful spirit
always will be everything
this was life
under the warmness of a rising sunshine
Tuesday afternoon, the collective will gather
and enter KPOO radio 89.5 FM
with our drums, flutes and our poetry
sharing our poetry
for The Poetry for the People Show
reflecting our time when Beat poetry
was living in its moment of joy
and at times we would perform
by Market and Powell streets
beside the cable car
I remember this past age
as time moves on
peace, love, and harmony
where every verse is a living poem
in our tradition of Beat poets and Diggers

Carlos Raúl Dufflar is a poet, playwright, and Founder and
Artistic Director of The Bread is Rising Poetry Collective,
which has performed in the US, Canada, and England. He
is, as of September 2023, a New Generation Lifetime Beat
Poet Laureate.

JEN DUNFORD-ROSKOS

don't go back

don't go back
and dance all night
to patsy cline

stay

light 2 cigarettes in unison in a cold motel room
where it doesn't matter,
the next morning,
if there are burn marks
on the sheets

Jen Dunford-Roskos hails from Providence, RI and
currently resides in Seaside Heights, NJ with her husband,
poet/publisher Dave Roskos. Her latest publication is a
novella entitled Love Junkie. She works with children with
development disabilities and runs Legitimate Business
Press.

SANDRA FEEN

Dead Ends

Distracted, I call in too late
and my absence isn't excused.
Even so, when I show up
for Thursday's Grand Jury,
the court administrator
somehow already spread news with quick

efficiency to other jurors that Mom died
the morning before because
everyone either said or mouthed
a soft "sorry," while looking to pick lint
off their pants, and a thick, awkward
kindness surrounds me for the duration.

I take meticulous notes
as I do for every indictment,
still mindful of instructions
to appear as if we are meeting a witness'
gaze, while in fact, direct eye contact is against

protocol. Then next witness
arrives, incriminating her son
for murder. She says it is her moral
duty, and as if in final thought, claims
her mothering has now vanished, and
tightens her grip on a handkerchief.

Air smells odd,
worst moment of silence
ever heard, as she straightens her posture,
steps down from deliberation.

I want to abandon rules,
meet her aching gaze
match desperation
but maintain duty to end.

Sandra Feen is the 2022-2024 Ohio Beat Poet Laureate. She designed a generative workshop on the history of the beat poetry movement with John Burroughs and presented it to members of the Ohio Poetry Association, in May. Author of three collections, she is currently editing an anthology You've Been Poemed: the 121 Project, and co-writing There is A Rock on Martin Avenue, with retired journalist and Pulitzer Prize winner, Cliff Treyens.

ROBERT FLEMING

clothes keep you naked

mother covered my hoochie coochie with nappies
at manhood commando
in a garden the pee pee cover is poison ivy
at fall leaves de-chloroform
from green to yellow to red to brown to
dust exposing thrusting under-brush
expose your garden germinator
skip fanny free from the garden to the city

Robert Fleming (b. 1963) is a word-artist born in Montreal, Quebec, Canada who emigrated to Lewes, Delaware, United States. Robert follows his mother as a visual artist and his grandfather as a poet. Robert is a founding member and contributing editor of Devil's Party Press' Old Scratch Press. https://www.facebook.com/robert.fleming.5030 .

Bryan Franco

Blame The Sun For The Rain

This rain, this
rain
banging on my window
pane
is messing with my
brain
is making feel
something other than
sane
or maybe not so
plain
I feel like whooping
like a whooping
crane
whoop…whoop…whoop
or maybe chewing chewing gum
on a choo choo
train
traveling from the Cali coast
to the coast of
Maine.
This rain, this
rain
this early May
state of Maine
rain
drip…drip...dripping
drop…drop...dropping
flipping and flopping
like flip flops flipping…flopping
all over the
place
taunting cucumbers and tomatoes
to rise from the ground
so we can
make
icy-coldy gazpacho

on sweltering hot,
sunny July and August
days
while thinking maybe
we could use a little more
rain
that might drive us
insane
but this rain, this rain, this
rain
is only water,
pieces of clouds
falling from the sky
pitter pattering against
spinning rooster weather
vanes
pounding on rooves
clang…clang
…clang
making us feel
like we need
to get out of the house
but we don't want to drive in it
but then
again
it makes us hungry
and no one wants
to cook on a rainy
day
so it teases us
by becoming heavier,
throwing
lightning in the air,
whips
around a little wind,
screams
with thunder
but it decides to not
stay
to move on and make its
way

to taunt someone else
in some other
place
only after the sun
pays
what the rain charges the sun
when it needs
to take itself
a break.

Bryan Franco is a gay, Jewish poet from Brunswick, Maine.
He has been published in the US, Australia, England,
Germany, Holland, India, Ireland, and Scotland. He won
the 2023 NAMI NJ Expressive Arts Mental Health Poetry
Contest and was a finalist in 2022 and is a Best Of The Net
nominee. He has facilitated poetry workshops for Brunswick
High School, Tumblewords Project, and Phynnecabulary.
He hosts Café Generalissimo Open Mic, is a member of the
Beardo Bards of the Bardo poetry troupe, painter, sculptor,
gardener, and culinary genius. His book "Everything I Think
Is All in My Mind" was published in 2021.

MATTHEW FREEMAN

Another Scribbler

When I told Beatnik Bob
that for many years my Clozaril
had wrecked my sex
drive he wasn't surprised.
"They don't want people like you
reproducing," he indicated.

I might wander Delmar Blvd. disconsolate
and come home to my efficiency
and have a can of mixed vegetables
for dinner all alone.
I do still believe
that I'm the exception
keeping civilization alive.

Matthew Freeman's seventh book of poems, I Think I'd
Rather Roar, was just published by Cerasus Poetry. He
holds an MFA from the University of Missouri-Saint Louis.
His awards are too numerous to mention here.

DAYNA GENEVIEVE

The Wait

a 1972 tattoo
Shiva blue

I've lost my longing piece for you

it feels good
ascending to the burn off point

the wild Mustangs mountainside ride
down

Náhuatl prayer

absolute absolvement

in the shadows
a victorian side show
rowdy tramps gather
the light

the angry and the arrogant
do me a favor won't cha?

I never start out trying to say anything
we enter worlds

it's a little better than
a bullshitty mind seeking adventure hokum

sex and drugs
grit and grime
time
travel
road weary warrior stories
setting off cock pistols in the desert
an ambient circus

Ry Cooder tune

till the carrion time comes

blood on their lips
as you search the sweetgrass
for reminders
a locket of photos and feathers

sleeping on a stone bed
decorated with flowers
waiting for the pilgrims to kneel at your frail feet

Dutch Treat
Cinnamon Girl
Amsterdam Secrets

there's a harbor of swaying red lipped hip ships
in tomorrow's window front

canalizing into tales

I tire of the dark stories
mine most of all

backstage lights
high as a kite
we gather our gang
and our ecstasy

dolling out turquoise beads
under shroud of
antique batik

electric blue leather
dusters
sweep
pointed corner polyester

huddled voices
raise their chins

singing out

"wait a minute Chester!"

Dayna Genevieve lives and hosts happenings on her ranch in Northern California

ANTHONY GEORGE

finding my mind

finding my mind
sometimes it falls out my pocket
and i have to search the streets
i found it once sleeping on the f train

i can find it engorged with fantasy dreams or rage
sloshing with tears hopes remorse and empty plates
wandering in the rain
burning and freezing season to season
sometimes my mind invents another mind
puts it to work and collects a fee for services

finding my mind
crawling up legs
growling under beds
burning breakfast
yelling in a quiet place
chasing the wind
taking a shit in the corner

i gave you my mind
you didn't give it back for years
i asked and demanded
i called i wrote letters
i sent mutual acquaintances
you laughed and finally gave it back
after your ratings dropped and you thought
there was nothing left

others who helped me lose my mind
gave me maps i trusted less and less
i never got to tell them how long it took
to conjure something out of ambiguity
to walk where i planned
to find people the way i remembered them
finding my mind wasn't so easy then
when i had traveled so far for everything else

74

and was everything but something for myself

Anthony George writes about dreams, angels, and ghosts and dead people and flesh and yelling and time. His recent books include finding my mind (iniquity press) and saint frankenstein (cat in the sun press). His poems have appeared in Misfit and Nerve Cowboy, among other cool publications.

CHRISTOPHER T. GEORGE

Shell Game

Venus, dear, I've elected
to play your shell game,
slap my cards on the table,
face side up (no doubt,
a dead man's hand).

Does your lustrous shell
contain a priceless pearl
or a useless grain of sand?

Grandma told me I will
have to eat a peck of dirt
before I die. Your shell
tantalizes and annoys me
like Shelley Berman, Shelley
Winters, and Shell gasoline.

Percy Bysshe Shelley had
it right, way back then:

Life's a shell game, we'll
either win or we'll lose.
It's not going well today.
Break out the booze.

Artwork: Sandro Botticelli, "The Birth of Venus"
circa 1485-6, Uffizi Gallery, Florence.

Christopher T. George was born in Liverpool, England, in
1948 and first came to the United States in 1955. He
studied poetry with Sister Maura Eichner and Elliott
Coleman. Chris's poetry has been published worldwide. He
has a poetry site at http://chrisgeorge.netpublish.net/

MIMI GERMAN

Starvation Peak

traded the mortar of hope the color of desert
blooms
to get on the horse to walk the ridge

skies above blown-out tires and jugs of piss
ridge high
above the hiss of slither

you can see where the sun is made
where the milky way beckons you
to drink its petals

i am a redwing blackbird singing
to the reeds and weeds
that grow these waters

i conjured this road
this holy dinghy
this one-paddled canoe

on starvation peak
i bit the juicy peach
drip

and saw the scam of preachers
cowering beneath
bleachers

through this chiseled rock
this earth
where once a buddha sat

where once
i was the bird
that sang into my hand

where once i was

the lone tree
where once i was the snow

where now i walk
through the valley
of the ancestors

un alone
and home
far

from the cities with their certain
brand of brick-walled misery
in the down town

in the briny thoughts of poets
and tin can shanties
lonelier than a field of concrete

Mimi German is the author of Beneath the Gravel Weight of
Stars. She resides in the wilderness of Oregon. The National
Beat Foundation named her Oregon's Beat Poet Laureate
for 2023-2025. Her poems have been published
internationally.

JANE 'SPOKENWORD' GRENIER

Flux

For my teacher who resides on a moon.
Busy contemplating contemplations
that shape the reality of a dimensional self.
Reminders of illusionary tactics of the mind
to keep you in line
dull your shine.
Spirit beings summoned by dreams
dancing to the songs of celestial bodies
listening to winds whispering the silent secrets.
Naked minds with no dressing as the dreamer's moon
laughs at my back.
Ruby sparkled sky laid out on a velvet sea
summon the moon and sweet talk the sun.
Dreaming of yesterdays and Saturn's' rings diamond snow
and strings spinning theories of planks
that travel on a shimmer
of not too long-ago memories.
Triangle suns born of stories told,
holes in time
and pharaohs lost to days of old,
I kissed the sky with rainbows gold.
In the book of pages, passed down from the lie
brary of ages, eons of particles appear and disappear,
expanding the nothingness
of a consciousness
long forgotten.
When night falls down upon us,
the beginning of the end
of the beginning
of the end of the beginning…we are allies
in the silent struggle.

Jane 'SpokenWord' Grenier wields her pen like a warrior's sword, she brings her artistry to a diverse set of venues from museums and clubs to busking street corners and living rooms everywhere. She has 2 published books and has been included in several anthologies. Her performances and collaborations include; Avant-Garde Maestro Cecil Taylor (AAJ best of 2016,) Nuyorican Poet Miguel Algarin, Beat poet/political activist John Sinclair, HipHop musician/ producer DJ Nastee & her partner in all things Albey onBass. https://janespokenword.com

FIN HALL

Rain Dogs

The past never stops chasing
Whenever you look, it's always there
Prisoners chat and gay Chinese play Mahjong, losing to the
man with longer hair
While mum and the man smoke black cigarettes on high rise
walkways.
Iris doesn't want to know her mum is a whore
And the proud perv paints pictures of vaginas

They set off to the big house in a silver Jaguar
August comes, they live a wonderful lie in otherwise idyllic
times
Like the Breath of a Sudanese rent boy
After a day trip to the farmers' market
Only lasting a few months before it got too much
Before having to go home to the family
And that didn't work out well did it?

Meanwhile Gloria the undertaker celebrates uncertainty by
spraying water
As Iris takes selfies with the dead,
Speaking of
The pool water filter may get clogged up with the suicide
victim who died pursuing his hobby
Attempting to kill himself, the poor man drowned twice now
"Here's your chance to love him," she says, after she came
to collect her things

In a refuge now, with neighbours that may have William
Morris wallpaper & a room for shoes
Live, laugh and love gets torn down and is now living under
the bunk beds
Murderers come with smiles, but the government pays £600
a week to keep you there
Lying on packets of pasta at the food-bank for a fiver
Collecting money online, is no crime

Day 29 in the funny farm, but it isn't that movie.

Dressing up, tarted up for the doctor
 Then getting turned away. Two wines over lunch does that
Rooms collapse, she runs out with a cross.
Jesus hasn't helped you this time although
he loves a hustler.
And even the police didn't flinch as she cursed at pashmina.
And the fireman helped them to safety
Before they left to see if there was a God in Skegness

Saccharine wank escaping from the fog with the juicy bone
Listening to voicemails
569 days sober, with the untouched wine in you hands
Crying, fed up of lying, sitting with her favourite pervert in an
art gallery
Waiting to get bigger than Dickens
All you can ask for in life is one moment of perfection

My name is Tennessee, Hell isn't as bad as it as it appears.
The internet says you're a bit of a dick, darling.
The job is yours. You start tomorrow
Kids play in broken ice cream vans
Simon says you've got to do something that scares you
once a day
But the internet is not a real place
Except for David Beckham of the Walworth Road.

When the authentic working class gets dropped because
she is authentic working class
This is not an exit: It's a road trip with a deviant and drunk
driver
The one with a baby on her bladder
Be on guard as time slips away so fast
I've seen the sky in fire , while cities burned to the ground.
But it's bleak out there
£7 and the tie back.
Lennie has a hard on, playing dead in the back seat
You pour wine and write a suicide note,
when Iris is at the beach
Head down the 70's blue toilet

Saved by the hand of the man who goes to the asylum for
two minutes

Aged 36. Too young to be perfect
Henry Miller was 44 when he first got published, Bukowski
was 55
But did they all lived happily ever after?

Fin Hall, AKA Like A Blot From The Blue, has work in
print in over 40 different publications in China, India, USA,
Canada as well as UK. and about 10 online. Including 2
solo collections He is also a filmmaker, performer, producer,
publisher, actor and collaborative artist. He has appeared in
various podcasts and radio stations. His latest collection is
called Headspace. Which is a collaboration with his
daughter Janine Rae and 15 year old granddaughter, Arya
Rae.

PAULA HAYES

Andy Warhol, A Life In Postcards

(Postcard 1)

An-dri-u Var-hol-a   Immigrant family
From the Carpathian Mountains   Villager
Father worked in coal mines   From Slovakia to Pittsburg
As though working class is not hard enough
Death takes away the father   when Andy is just thirteen

A mother did what she could
Went into other people's homes
to clean what wasn't hers   And what she didn't own
They say Andy was sickly as a child
Read a lot of movie magazines

Shirley Temple signed a glossy   Holy relic of seeing the
screen
His name spelled wrong on it

But a boy grows up   1949 finds New York
Just the way it is

Things can't always stay like that

Commercial artists get paid
1960's   the dawning of new fads
Andy one of the most expensive

(Postcard 2)

The Abstract Expressionists
Were all like a bunch of walking Charles Bukowski's

John Jaspers, and his lover, Robert Rauschenberg
Andy wanted at least John
or did he want Rauschenberg?
Hell, did he want them both?
Hard headed, hard core alcoholics, hard living, hard loving
84

And their art was the only god they worshiped

1958   Jaspers' "Flag" paintings,   Castelli Gallery
Art world freaked Over some star and stripes
Over some red and white   Shit, some blue

They were all too eager   Mad in their own desires
Not raging, but raging
Holding the pain of pills and booze
Like hands of lovers
Lost but not in solitude
New York,   Sick with mist,   gray and opaque
Splash some paint over it
Before the world is fatigued

"You are too swish," Andy."
You are just too damn swish for them.
But what is swish if not posh
and what is posh if not another word for fuck
And what's wrong with a little commercial success, anyway?

(Postcard 3)

When you are you   That upsets people
And creation of yourself
Is harder to master than people think
When you make yourself into your own myth

Andy needed a studio   He couldn't go on forever
stacking paintings on Lexington Avenue
His mother's house

And when you have a need   Like an addict searching for
a fix
You become vulnerable to your own thirst and hunger

Andy was a myth already   Sensitive outcast
Pouring on   Irving Blum
saw all the soup can paintings on Lexington Avenue
On the floor   the paintings lay, positioned
above the paintings was a photograph of Marilyn Monroe

Blum knew how a man so in need
Could be made to see what he saw
Take Andy's desire   and teach Andy
how to project his own desire
so that we are all desiring
What we never knew we wanted

The photograph was nothing really
Just a sheet of paper torn out of a magazine
More pop   Pinned up on the wall
Blum offered to take Andy to LA
But Andy wanted a NY gallery

Blum took Andy by the arm
And whispered over his ear, "Movie stars" will see it
In the city of Angels,
pointing to Marilyn's image

And just like that Andy in LA

(Postcard 4)

Yes, it happened   The Soup Can Exhibition
FERUS Gallery, Los Angeles   Andy's first exhibition
32 SOUP CANS   This was POST-WAR LA ART
Thank you Irving Blum   Thank you Andy

1962

Finally.....

Some motion. Just a blink. Marisol blinked.
Because desire can never be held forever
And desire can never stand still
Sooner or later one or the other lovers moves
Shifts

Desire cannot be held in tension forever
Sooner or later

No matter how prolonged desire may be
Just like that   in the blink of an eye
Desire changes.

The film, Kiss, 1963.

Paula Hayes is a poet hanging out in Memphis, the same town where the ghost of Elvis roams in the jungle room of Graceland. Since music imbibes her soul and the blues are sometimes her muse, it seems a natural fit to call this city home.

RICHARD WAYNE HORTON

ARRANGEMENT FOR THREE CAFE POEMS

In the poet café a woman smiled at me.
The wind ruffled her hair.
She turned to her journal and wrote, "Oh, Joy!
I'm young! I'm young! I'm young!"

In the poet café a hand kept waving.
Across the table a head kept nodding.

In the poet café a gust of wind
blew papers into the street.
The poet popped up in consternation.

In the poet café a table needed cleaning.
A sparrow's twig legs hopped over fries, tasty lumber.
Then the bird lit on the sandwich and savaged it.
Get at the meat of the poem and draaaaaaag it out.
That's right! That's the payload right there!

Across the street in the church,
the priest struggled to turn a page,
and found himself rising with a terrible lightness
to regions unknown.
The balcony began floating away.
But a saint stayed behind, snagged in a window
of doubt.
The choir made lovely sandwiches of sound,
while the sun ignited the church front like an A-bomb.

A raised hand released the worshippers,
and they gathered in the door's shadow,
till it swung wide and pigeons dived,
with murder on their mind.

The wind took a church leaflet
on a journey high over the city.

Pilgrims crossed a river of cars
to the breakfast joint which swam
in a brown beverage of shadow.
Inside, their voices cranked and settled
at the construction site of their breakfast plates.

Somewhere there was a high window,
where a watcher laughed, but cried too,
as dirty little gods walked the street below.
Colossal worlds veered drunkenly
beneath an unfair traffic light,
and a clock hand that had fallen off the tower
was cutting off all escape.
Near the watcher's bed the next dream
waited patiently for his return.

Across town, accordions were marching down Main street,
dancing as they played. One held a flag.
But they were hungry, those accordions.
That wasn't good.

They entered the café where we sit now,
watching them come in.
They saw the merrymakers here and wished to join us!
Welcome, accordions!

Everyone looks up and smiles.
Mom smiles. Dad smiles. Grandma smiles.
Grandpa smiles. The children smile.
The smiling cook. The smiling dish washer.
All the smiling customers!

Even the lovers in the corner, oh, you lovers!
We saw you kissing just now,
as the accordions played!

Do you know what time it is?
It's time for a celebration!
Up goes the confetti!
Up go the balloons!
Up go the petticoats!

Oh, my accordions! Bringing back the old country!

Not leaving, are you?
Come back to us again!

They were at the door, but they've stopped!
They're turning around! They're coming back in!
ONE… MORE… TIME!!!
Dance! Dance! Dance! My fingers!
On the keys of my accordion!
Can-can fingers! Tango fingers! Wildly dancing fingers!
Play us a tune! Oh! Play that melody again!

They must have heard, because they've stopped!
They smile at each other! The raised baton!
They're playing it again! My favorite melody!

I'm in tears! Give me your handkerchief!
It's wet already! Give me another one!
That fellow's not crying!
Let's steal his handkerchief! Oh, what a prank!
He needs a good slap with a wet handkerchief!
A thousand wet handkerchiefs!
Slapping a thousand serious faces!
Slapping friends! Slapping total strangers!
Slap!   Slap!   Slap!
Everybody's slapping each other!

What a funny night at the cafe!

Richard Wayne Horton has received 2 Pushcart nominations and is the 2019-21 MA Beat Poet Laureate. His work has appeared in Southern Pacific Review, Scryptic, Lonesome October Lit, The Dead Mule, Meat For Tea, Bull & Cross, Danse Macabre du Jour and others. He has published 4 books: Sticks & Bones (2017), Artists In The Underworld (2019), Ballet For Murderers (2021) and Artists In The Underworld, 2023 Edition (2023).

KATHLEEN HULSER

Blood and Ashes

The difference between blood and ashes
Blood is burnt sienna
whereas ashes are burnt bones.
Blood speaks in bubbles and giggles
a swift current of merriment.
Ashes mumble, hugging their gloom
weighted with memories.

Blood bursts and flows, sticks and clots,
masquerades as lining and surface –
   the transparent overcoat of shy skin.
Ashes flaunt their grace,
drifting, swooping like swallows,
sketching faces on the wind.

Blood knows only the present
while time crushes ash
pressing it into bricks, stacked solid.
Liquid blood pulses hot and cold
even as stolid ashes know no weather.
The urn's libation may pour
gently through a dust cloud of ash,
mixing all that once was forever.

Kathleen Hulser is a writer, public historian, and activist
involved in the arts and history. She has been curator at
the Museum of the American Gangster, and NY Transit
Museum, New-York Historical Society public historian and
has taught American History at NYU, New School and Pace.
Significant shows include Slavery in NY and Petropolis:
A Social History of Animal Companions. She also creates
activist art projects and walking tours such as Bad, Rad and
Boho Women of the Village. Her "I Don't Write Poetry and
You Can't Make Me" is forthcoming from Press22
Publishing.

PATRICK HUNTER

It's Hard to Mosh When
Your Hips Hurt

It's hard to mosh when your hips hurt,
Johnny Rotten had a reality show
called Rotten TV and Joe Strummer
has been gone for almost twenty years
I'm a fifty-seven-year-old punk putting together
IKEA furniture with names like
Äpplarö, Björksta, Knutstorp
where did all the Anti-Pasti, Hüsker Dü
and Sham 69 go?
Yagerbombs with junk chasers
and anarchy have been replaced
with yard work and gardening
I enjoy planting peonies,
the trick is to plant them in the early fall
or spring when the soil is warm
and all my power cords sound like,
"Hey, you kids, get off of my lawn,"
filled with the same intensity and angst.
Our moppets are young adults now
and I explain the artistic temperament to them,
but they are off doing their own thing
with new ideas about life and acceptance
they call me an aging hipster; I'd prefer
Johnny Thunders, but I can live with that.

Patrick Hunter has been writing poetry and short stories for over 35 years. His works have appeared in several independent journals and publications, including Caufield, Red Words, Love's Executive Order and Beat Generation. Patrick has an MBA and an MM from McGill University and has studied poetry independently with American Poet Matthew Lippman. Patrick's debut book of poems, "Raw Eggs", will be published by Friesen Press this upcoming fall.

MARCUS IF

red thread sutra
(after Ikkyu

picking stockings from the floor red thread everyday wash
jubilant zen hauling water mindful fucking
cutting wood this stiff erection
pissing in the boardroom
ejaculating about town
hot enticement physical extravagance what Law
if not our own   ,   natural
law of urges
the dharma between her legs or bottom
of a workingman's pint.

smoke of imagination the first thread of magic
our tangible flesh   woven stars   fabric of the multiverse
attachment uncalculated   :   the diamond razor's edge
        -   it boogies -
primitive undulations the first drug you ever   loved
the last orgasm you'll ever need
unraveled.

Marcus If is a performance poet (not Slam) that has been
active on the Colorado Front Range for over 30 years. In
2012 he founded the Beyond Academia Free Skool in
Boulder as a 100% free peer-to-peer literary collective. He
is also known as the operator of the 70-ton Steam Shovel in
Nederland CO, as an anarcho-syndicalist community
organizer, lead vocals/washboard for the Jug Shovel band,
and Zen Tyrant of Love Shovel Ranch in Nederland. Mr.
If may be the epitome of the autodidactic redneck, having
been ejected from every school he ever attended and yet
still inventing such notables as the Projective Sonnet,
Ontological Engineering, and the Nose Rake. His spirit
animal is the werewolf.

DANE INCE

Done did it again

All that is left
of Sappho's songs
Some say nothing just dust
Not different from professor's
Cussing memories
Vomit out loud couplets on the rusty dented yellow school
bus
Your starched plaid pleated cotton dress saturated with the
smell of wood smoke fire
I like you like a goddess over the altar of the Pacific
I like you in black
I like you on the patio veranda
Your visage steals my words and I am lost and blank
Staring at the zigzag bricks on the floor
Wishing
Yes wishing
I could take your hand in mine
The picture shows me cold and gray
Wish we were walking down and away in silent seagull
gliding fashion to seashore sand
You playful in green dress joy on playground
You in the corner of the shed
Holding baby donkey close
Melts me into a dream of tomorrow
But I wake up
And I am dead
Everywhere there is the terror
The old movies of war
Broadcast to slipping chip implants just behind the tin tinned
flap
Just behind the ears
Egads
What have we done
Gone and done
Done did it again
Quick throw out the parachutes
All the dead weight

We are a goner
If we cannot get lighter
Levitate
The plane is stuttering
Shells streaming by
The plane is sinking
Throw out all the extra weight
Even those bad ideas are too heavy
Throw everything out
The plane is sinking
Or else we will be lost!
There is no future
None at all for a 1930s bit player
Hidden lost
In the background flicker of a Buster Crabbe serial
Utter despair on the day
On this day of the passing
Flash Gordon is no more

Dane Ince is an internationally published poet, hosts a weekly open mic "Time to Arrive", Beat Poet Laureate for California 2022-2024, and publisher at EYEPUBLISHEWE. COM. Dane is a producer of online events such as a poetic gathering of writers from around the world in support of Ukraine. His first collection of poetry was published in October 2022 titled "The Whole Existential Novel; the journey from the darkside of the rainbow to Satchidananda"

CATHERINE KATEY JOHNSON

Old Is Fast

You got a new car
hood full of horses
face jammed against your skull
when pedal meets plush pile.
But that's slo-mo, friend
'cause old comes at cha fast.

It slams you into a brick wall
two-thirty in the morning.
You're about to wet the bed
so, you hurry to the bathroom.
Man, that's a trip
'cause the five meds they got you on
give you the Tilt-a-whirl dizzies,
but you gotta' get there fast
and you do
whirling lightning
that's you
old real fast.

Dancing at the Prom yesterday
now you're stirring
fiber in your juice.
Coughed up a piece of lung
before toes hit floor.

At the Casino, you realize
your insurance is a gamble, too.
You're betting you'll die,
become dismembered, or worse.
How the hell do you win that bet--
that bet against the temple?
And that stupid chin hair
comes back every thirty-minutes!
Jewelry box replaced
with old people trinkets
thermometer, BP cuff, hearing-aid,

moleskin toe pads,
corn removers, wart-off,
magnifying glass, gel pads,
Icy-Hot patches, things to make you go,
things to make you stop,
medicated pads,
pads to catch the drips, flashlight,
tweezers for that damn chin hair.
All of it piles high overnight
'cause old happens fast.

Your Mr. T starter kit
all says "Medic Alert"
Diabetic,
Pacemaker,
Allergic to Ibuprofen,
Percoset,
Darvon,
Penicillin,
Laytex,
and cherries;
on Aspirin,
on Norvasc,
on HCL, Zoloft,
on Glucophage and Niaspan,
on Donner, on Blitzen--
shit, what was I saying?
Oh, yeah, old is fast.

Titanium frames your blind eyes
binds your bones together.
Blood pressure's up, pulse is down
so the Pacemaker zaps you forty-four percent
of every twenty-four/seven.
You went in for a sleep test
when sex probably would have fixed it
and came out with a Zippo sized lump
above your left tit
That happened fast.
Is that Raquel Welch on CSI?
Damn, I hope I look that good at seventy-one.

All I know is
it'll be here in a minute.

And him over there, not any better.
His arteries get real hard.
If only he could use his arteries to--
he sets the TV tray aside to go get the mail
knees knocking into his man apples.
We're old and we got here fast.

*First Published in Fifty Shades of Gray Hair. This
poem was voted most entertaining poem at the
Oklahoma State Fair.

Katherine Katey Johnson - Award-winning New
Generation Beat poet, Woody Guthrie Poet and Oklahoma
Poet. Her collections are Fifty Shades of Gray Hair, a
tangled collectionband Resting Soil, neither of which have
numbered pages because in Oklahoma women don't count.

STRIDER MARCUS JONES

THE HEAD IN HIS FEDORA HAT

a lonely man,
cigarette,
rain
and music
in a strange wind blowing

moving,
not knowing,
a caravan
whose journey doesn't expect
to go back
and explain
why everyone's ruts have the same
blood and vein.

the head in his fedora hat
bows to no one's grip
brim tilted inwards
concealing his vineyards
of lyrical prose
in a chaos composed
to be exposed,
go, git
awed
and jawed
perfect and flawed,
songs from the borderless
plain
where no one has domain
and his outlaw wit
must confess
to remain

a storyteller
that hobo fella

a listening barfly

for a while,
the word-winged butterfly
whose style
they can't close the shutters on
or stop talking about
when he walks out
and is gone.

whiskey and tequila
with a woman who can feel ya
inside her, and know she's not Ophelia
as ya move as one,
to a closer and simplistic,
unmaterialistic
tribal Babylon,

becomes so,
when she stands, spread
all arms and legs
in her eskimo
Galadriel glow,
sharing mithril breath,
no more suburban settlements
and tortured tenements
of death,
just a fenceless forest
and mountain quests
with a place to rest
on her suckled breasts,
hanging high, swinging slow.

warped clouds HARP
through stripped leaves and bark,
where bodies sleeping in houseboat bones
reflect and creak in cobbled stones:
smokey sparks from smoked cigars
drop like meteorites from streetlight stars,
as cordons crush civil rights
under Faust's fascist Fahrenheit's.

one more whiskey for the road.
another story lived and told
under that
fedora hat
inhaling smoke
as he sang and spoke
stranger fella
storyteller.

Strider Marcus Jones–poet, law graduate, civil servant from England with proud Celtic roots in Ireland and Wales. He is the editor and publisher of Lothlorien Poetry Journal. A Poetry Society member, his five published poetry books reveal a maverick, roaming cities, tooting his sax in smoky rooms. https://lothlorienpoetryjournal.blogspot.com/. https://stridermarcusjonespoetry.wordpress.com/

RESCUEPOETIX
SUSAN JUSTINIANO

WE KEEP GOING

How do we trust the voices that we hear?
Stories told from the lens of privilege… are they without bias?
The narrative guilty of erasure told from where
continuing lies feed back into mock righteousness

There are moments we find ourselves looking for something,
end up finding trauma disguised as tradition
in places we least expect or from those coming
breathing falsehoods by omission

Times we try to escape our own lives,
casting blame on others
Looking away from ourselves,
suffering inherited through bloodlines
Struggling to keep the happily ever after we signed up for
Deserving better than to live in darkness

But
no one can run that fast
We're told we don't stand a chance
And yet here we are
We stand
We break
We keep going

No longer running, hiding in the shadows,
away from ourselves
Breaking instead of being broken; the lies, the trauma,
 the malintent
Redefine slowly, rebuilding, more than as fraught survivors
Sharing voices and stories of living,
come back joyful and content

Those who keep coming back are the unbeatable ones
Unlocking what binds us
Thriving in the chaos, living over and over, building new bonds
Writing our new story backwards

RESCUEPOETIX - Susan Justiniano, the first Puerto Rican woman Poet Laureate Emeritus of Jersey City, NJ and State of New Jersey Beat Poet Laureate (2022-2024), is a bilingual globally published performing poet, advocate, spoken word artist, recording artist and teaching artist. She established her professional artist brand, RescuePoetix™ and is an arts advocate deeply involved in the arts community since 2006 and currently serves on the boards of several arts organizations throughout the USA. https://linktr.ee/rescuepoetix

DESPINA KALPAKIDOU

Why do you keep me in silence?

Why do you keep me in silence?
I need your replay
To feel your presence
To imagine your face
As white as angelic …

Your beautiful lips
to penetrate my mouth
Deeply and sensually
But don't raise my hopes, my love
Only to let them fall down.

The sound of your silence's deafening
Like interlocking stones,
it seems Opening, closing,
dissolving bodies
Scattering my fragile dreams …

Let me soar high, my love,
Don't cast me down as a weight.
Keep me alive in your embrace ,
And together, we'll defy fate!

Lyrics by Despina Kalpakidou #deskal

Despina Kalpakidou comes from Greece. She was born in
Athens and now lives and works in Larissa. She works as
a teacher and her involvement with language and literature
made her aware and gave her the tools to write poems and
articles. The source of inspiration is nature, human
relationships and social issues. She has recently published a
poetry collection with the title 'Dreams and Loves of a Youth".
She is married and has three children.

ALSHAAD KARA

"Never die tomorrow"

When the sun sets,
The moon rises.

In between, there is an eclipse,
That no on talks about,
Where we both met.

Which is found,
On the verge
Of pain and obituaries,
Full of solitude,

Resulting in an intense refuge
Of love.

Until one shall unwind the winds,
Which hides the shells
Of sheer selfishness.

That no sleep can uncover
The surprise
Of being together
In that moment,
During this eclipse.

"Madness of love"

My heart is breaking,
I can feel it...
Inside, my heartbeat is boiling
With blood...

Am I finished,
Because of an obsession
Regarding this eternal madness?

My heart is breaking,
I can feel it...

All I miss,
Is your heat next to my heart.

Break our courtship,
As per courtesy
In this celebration of love...

My heart is breaking,
I can feel it on the butcher block.
Into massive heartbreaks,

All because of a mad love...

Alshaad Kara is a Mauritian poet who writes from his heart. He won the Gal's Guide Anthology 2023 People's Choice Award for his poem "Prelude". His latest poems were published in two anthologies, "Gal's Guide Anthology: Journey" and "Suicide Vol.2", one magazine, "The Ryder Magazine April/May 2023" and two journals, "Literary Cognizance Vol.- III, Issue- 4, March 2023" and "Cultural Reverence Vol. V; No. 2; April 2023".

Karlostheunhappy (aka Carl Spiby)

AFTER ROBERT BRIGGS #3

rising up now - a next-Gen Beat Generation
outlaw poetics of new millennia:

sure, we look back over the sunflower tenements
over moonlit railroads, its boxcars, boxcars, boxcar butterfly
cargo of beat stanzas

sure, we look back over the sunflower tenements
over bebop minds laid bare there, washed up in the beer
froth of the roaring
Pacific waves that trace 'round this cruel & dying world
globalised now with techways ripe for revolution, reclamation

sure, we're out to trap new lines Ginsberg-Blakean
hang them out fresh, out there hanging in the mindtree
prophetic phrases of gold evening & the night that slides
under days of pain

sure, we look on to the possible future before us & the
swirling nowdeath-life
of moment, this song of this death life lifting the lid on the
forgotten heart
scoop with a sigh under heavy rocks to gaze at the stars that
glow there
gathering as new children of the universe & celebrate
Kerouac at 100
each year the Goddesses
celebrate ourselves, Whitman-like!

'you're just reading the news!'
someone accused next-Gen Beat lifetime laureate PAUL
RICHMOND

'it's just a list of things'
someone called out to little ol Karlostheunhappy as I raged
thru a HYDROGEN JUKEBOX of the German songs of
sorrow, houseless

the No House Row & death shadowed easily on the streets,
lined there right on the streets, like a list of things...

Ah, dear 'someone': you have to play your own part in this
tune, friend
you have to walk with us in the burning stanzas
dance w/us to music of time, fall upon stillness of moment –

SO COME ON IN, friend; don't linger at the edge
look! the others are already in the sea –

in that review, I tried to find reality in the cardboard streets
'under the gravel weight of stars' because Mimi's the
grit-queen, keen honest words true and to do so thru lens of
word song stanzas which – let's face it – is spine of all poetry
afterall, isn't it?

so, I guess we fall failed if readers can't see (or, worse, won't)
–
in our defence, this mess of wordage is always a compromise
on reality...
all we can do is hope minds take a moment & kick up the
leaves
rescue some fresh fallen thought –

News..? DANE INCE … California laureate
he got the news
O! Captain, My Captain GEORGE WALLACE
he got the news
- the ghost of WALT WHITMAN knows your soul, friend,
fellow traveller of stanza songlines –

RON WHITEHEAD - warlock of the scene
he got the news
got it right from chief correspondent: the DOCTOR –
MICHAEL SINDLER
have your read his write that lives in the neon nest we call the
cosmos?

Deb says: This ain't 'just' the news, it IS THE NEWS!
Come see! Hear these pages of sweat unholy beatitude
108

come wander in these waves of blue blues leaf-pages
come walk wandering these cries of great street soul,
my congregation & friends
and don't forget yr shades…
chance the lightning: the news is that there's the highs of
high and
the blue mind sky is free for all and the low is you know.
Besides, outlook for the rest of the week is more of the
same:
entropy they call it.
So swim in the dying, dip into the dreams dear reader
(our readers: friends we call them).
Ah, if this is 'just the news' - words and unholy visions of the
holy
then our work here is DONE –

if that review is just a list spit of pain and grit-teethed kerbs
of blood
then our work here is DONE - done dear composers
of stars in the gutter asking what if the sun was really blue?
after all, all stars end –
such magic debris written, collected
by the Foundation, our Foundation
this gathering of friends lost in the living hot words, aching
eyes
we but the dancing dust of 14 billion years existence
not just the 4.5 we've been loitering here
loitering in the doorways of our own solitude
in the doorways of sunset sunrises
in the doorways of bars, bars, bars
quiet in the doorways of love, waiting to be let in, let in to the
hot glory night
w/words that give shadow the nod to love's awakening,
death & undeath
still loitering in the doorway of wondrous life
black letters hid hidden in the doorway shade of that poem
you wrote,
all of you, every one of you
& the underneath shadow too: we write beneath the
shadows of the moon
so, just so, – and this is it, as it is, as it is – to all, we give

thanks
we the dead writers of gold, of our sunken age
we who sing the sermon: BEATITUDE!
we who sing the sermon: be-at-itude

Karlostheunhappy: International Beat Poet Laureate (England) 2022-2023, Karlostheunhappy is the author of 'OBLIVION: 200 Seasons of Pain & Magic', available from Gloomy for Pleasure (gloomyforpleasure.com). He's also appeared in 'Beatdom' and 'International Times' and numerous anthologies. A second collection is due soon, plus a project with Portland's Mimi German and he's curated and edited an anthology 'BeatSurreal' also due later this year. Follow on facebook.com/karlostheunhappy.

JOE KIDD

I LIVE IN THE TREES

I live in the trees
from branch to branch
from city to city
I leap in the canopy, on this planet plantation
no grief, no guilt, no baggage to burden
just flesh and bone
and gravity to pull

I live in the trees
where the Jaguar and the Harpy lurk
with claws like a bear, and an appetite to match
my opposing thumbs and mental gymnastics
are but an appetizer
in this merciless chain

I live in the trees
with my children and family
we perch high atop the horror show
we sing and howl and dance in the rain
we will cleanse the sullen memory
of those crying and carried away

I live in the trees
with the fruit and the flower
fragrant and delicate
if just for a moment
up here where everything is mine
and we now understand
that we all die tomorrow

I live in the trees
that have long since fallen
to become soil and fertilizer and carbon fuel
organic beds where generations grow
and fossils once buried now expose in their sacrifice
a seed in softened mound
baked in the starlight until the heart finds it's beat

one day in eternity
timeless and free

I live in the trees
cut and formed
to shelter and comfort against the storm
a home, a sanctuary, a lasting monument
a hollow reed sings, a silent bell chimes
design of the artisan
work of the magician

I live in the trees
shaved and cleansed
lighter than air
thinner than skin
where I write these words on once living parchment
my ghost haunting forever on the dusty shelves
and my confession of love
to honor such poetry
to inhabit this paradise
on my knees

I live in the trees
in the gardens of the spheres
the moons and the Saturnites
where we all wear rings
the temples and the flags, trembling to the south
white flowers light the darkness
royal songs pollinate
feathers and skulls litter the landscape
indigo blood stains and crystallized tears
a holocaust of terror and DNA
patriarch and priest on an organic altar
where that blood becomes wine
for demons dehydrated
old gods devoured
unprotected by worship
new gods approach
in their vehicles and vessels
while we observe from on high
the chaos and calamity

and I continue
and I care not
I live in the trees

Joe Kidd is a working, published poet and songwriter. In 2020, published The Invisible Waterhole, a collection of spiritual and sensual verse. Awarded by the Michigan Governor's Office and the United States Congress. Joe is the current Beat Poet Laureate for the State of Michigan 2022/2024. Joe is a member of National & International Beat Poet Foundation, Angora Poets, 100 Thousand Poets For Change.

Author Page: https://www.amazon.com/Joe-Kidd/e/B089QYDXSM
Face Book Page: https://www.facebook.com/profile.php?id=100063704010587

PATTI BARKER KIERYS

MY DEAR FRIENDS

How blessed I am to have dear friends
that inspire me to be the best I can
never alone or in doubt
they are close to hear me out

Seeing me for who I truly am
encouraging me to share what I can
lifting me up when I feel broken
nothing is out of bounds or unspoken

Caring about each friend
listening to their every word
knowing they have wisdom
to help me live and learn

Though different in many ways
does not matter for you see
differences change as we share
friendship matters most to me

We laugh and cry over life's ups and downs
our friendship helps us find a way out
from times that get us down
going forward is what it's all about

May my friends hold me close in their hearts
as they are always held in mine
joy fills my life when thinking of them
each are a loving part of my life's journey

My dear friends are loving gifts I cherish
thankful for their care and guidance
they make me dance through life
happy, blessed and fulfilled

Love and hugs come my way
spirit keeps them close each day

my heart is full with their caring ways
no more need be said this day
except I LOVE YOU

Patti Barker Kierys is a woman of many interests. She is
an award winning artist, Reiki Master Teacher, author, poet
and photographer. Her creative passion and spiritual
inspiration can be seen in her poems, paintings, collage,
photography and inspirational messages. She writes ar-
ticles for the international organization Reiki Rays. Upon
retiring after 50 years in law, a surprising passion arose.
She began writing poetry and continues to enjoy it to this
day. She can be reached at pmkierys@att.net and on
Facebook - Patti Barker Kierys

DEBBIE TOSUN KILDAY

Memories... not all good

Memories
Of people I have known
Loved, and now gone

Some were blurry eyed
Filling a jigger
Laced with liquor
While having
Another whiskey nipper

Some flying high
Eyes bloodshot
All the while
Pharmaceutical company's stock
Soaring upwards
Towards the sky

Nick
Lighting up another
Black tar stick
After getting another fix
Thinking he's looking
Cool for the chicks

Never to be cured
Premiums climbing
I can make a bet
The banks will never let you
Get out of debt

Manipulated media
To make sure
you never hear the truth

Governments waging war
Another round of bullets
For peace

Sometimes I feel numb
Like I've lived too long

Memories… not all good
but a reminder
Of how far we have come.

Debbie Tosun Kilday is a Beat Poet, writer, award winning author, nature photographer, artist, illustrator, and owner/ CEO of the National Beat Poetry Foundation, Inc., it's Festivals, and New Generation Beat Publications. She is the author of several books, short stories and poetry. She has appeared on tv and radio. Debbie is a Connecticut native and resident.

ANTONIA ALEXANDRA KLIMENKO

That Cat Named Bird

Charlie"Bird" Parker, jazz legend, 1920-1955

He could have squeezed the living daylights out of Hell
And so he did   And at his very leisure
His euphoric appetite for bright pain and dulled pleasures—
hip-hopping, be-bopping   jammin' slammin'
pumping iron and ironic in metaphoric basements
where swinging trumpets blow— was legendary
His valves   those brass knuckles of brute sound
opened like delicate testicles (ah…the swell of it)
under the pressure of his well-manicured hand
Sometimes out of hand   But then   that was Birdland

He lived for…Oh, what he'd give for:
whole notes suspended from jazz-stained ceilings
ripping   renting   warbling   squealing A yardbird
desperate to fill the uncompromising space
His face   a black hole   where stars exploding
collapsed into fusion   replaced glass windows
shattered like melting mirrors from the Ice Age
Nineteen was a nice age   The kid had class
His Cherokee in B flat—pure synergy—
(unsurpassed) peeled poems off of every wall
drove a silk fist with a twist through blood knowledge
stripped down to the quick   Once he heard the call…

no one could keep that horn in its cage

Dawn and neon merging together echoed
his interpolations   Muted shades of strobing rhythms--
he was a language of collisions--a free fall
of featherless wings   Icarus caught in the wailing gale
the chromatic scale of stark illusion penetrating confusion
soft callused lips cut from the equinox of tonal
depth and fragile power   The cryptic
and unspoken lodged in his bill--a shuttered
windowsill opening into a symphony an epiphany
118

a sunflower smiling wide in the ache of his throat
The dark chords of his vocabulary—stuttering nocturnal–
perched now   in treetops   pronouncing his return

Melodies rose up through rampant leaves of invention
Green summer ferns   potted plants   rotted plants
April in Paris Bird Gets the Worm Ornithology (no apologies)
34 years of unearthly episodic breakups   breakdowns
stanza continued
a narcotic intervention gave him pause   but no rest
Melodies rose up through visions of greatness
sketches of Miles Monk and Dizzy
burnt bulbs eclipsing   distant strains mixing chaotic
in fresh saxophonic   kaleidoscopic   dimension

Pneumonia in half breaths   a heartfelt diminuendo
What was he thinking? This is it   maybe
This is the moment   this is the tone
this is the one sound I can really bring home
No more hot-lining liner notes for the final crescendo
Play me the sudden death of midnights Baby!
Play me the jazz-beaked Bird   that old deaf fool
Play me that one impossible screech of a cosmic sage
Blue on ebony   arpeggio of dreaming

No one could keep that horn in its cage!

And in one hush of morning, Destiny brushed
his dry parting lips   his unfettered hips
the suicidal longing of his cold wet drool
The wick of his short flame lit an interval higher
in a sky of blazing burnout—his fame gone cool
That formless ghost of his haunting moan–
his feathers clipped   nothing lost   nothing wanting
His music out the window   his notes off the page

No one could keep that bird in his cage!

ANTONIA ALEXANDRA KLIMENKO - Nominated multiple times for the Pushcart Prize, The Best of the Net and a former San Francisco Poetry Slam Champion, is widely published. She is the recipient of two grants: one from Poets in Need, of which Michael (100 Thousand Poets for Change) Rothenberg was a co-founder, the second—the 2018 Generosity Award bestowed on her by Kathleen Spivack for her outstanding service to international writers through SpokenWord Paris where she is Poet in Residence. Her collected poems, On the Way to Invisible is forthcoming in 2023.

DINAH KUDATSKY

I AM AFRAID

Would you sit with me? I'm afraid -
Afraid of summer's endless day, the aching,
slow beats of timeless time.
shadows moving along the wall.
Laundry flapping on a clothesline.
The knocking of Venetian blinds against the window.
The smell of too much green in the heat.
the itchy sound of cicadas.
The world is dangerous: wars are breaking out,
and those shards of broken glass are still on the kitchen
floor!
I am afraid: he's paying for his coffee, leaving the cafe,
the unmet lover;
I'll never see him again. Come back! talk to me!
Of women, with flat bellies,
and me moving through molasses,
to search for my own weird beauty
at the other end of this bad dream
Afraid of the unexpected smell of English Leather
on a stranger, returning me
to a slow dance with my first love, when we were young,
and of never being loved again.
I hide from neatly-dressed Evangelicals at my door, sincere
and relentless,
zombies smiling, come to save me from myself.
And women with sprayed Republican hair,
hard as Gestapo helmets
unmoving in the wind
Do you see that long fingernail, red and vicious, tapping a
freshly-lit Marlboro?
Those tendrils are coming for me, to replant the sweet hook
of addiction
And I am afraid of the world,
which will not hold up its end of things
even for a moment while I try to rest.

Hold my hand: I don't know which way to run,
like the squirrel
in the road, as the truck roars closer.
I rehearse my mother's inevitable death,
with each cardiac crisis,
flailing with grief, failing to be ready.
My father's face, in that funeral home, cold and stiff
unable to forgive me for being the girl he didn't want
I try to shut out the angry hum of fluorescent lights, dental
drills, mosquitoes
at a vein, and power plants.
And have you rounded a corner, suddenly face to face with
the deceitful
best friend now enemy, to see her, still alive?
Protect me! From high tension wires! Skulls and crossbones
on bottles!
The fake smiles of store clerks on commission!
Thunder! The pledge of allegiance!
Being called to the front of the room!
Resumés! Weddings, window treatments, table settings!
Pleasantries! Earnest and heartfelt sing-alongs!
Clitoridectomies!
Official-looking envelopes in the mail!
My echoing footsteps in a marbled courthouse!
The long night alone! The long drive to the hospital,
not breathing!
Hallmark holidays! Patriotism! Clowns, magicians, balloons,
parades!
The smell of antiseptic soap in White Castle,
between nowhere and nowhere!
The rehearsed and dead voice of the telemarketer!
Endless touch-tone menus! Muzak when you've been left on
hold and forgotten!
And saleswomen, who insist on knowing how I am today,
when I'm out of Xanax
I am afraid of dark halls with burnt out light bulbs
and muffled shouting behind doorways.
Cracked linoleum and the smell of overcooked cabbage.
I am afraid it will be discovered that I've been impersonating
a normal person.
I am afraid of never being known!

And yes, of this white sheet before me, seeking a writer
with a personal reference from God, yet only I showed up
I am afraid that you and I were using a phone made of tin
cans and string,
like in the nineteen-fifties, and I've been talking to you all
night,
but you've put your can down, gone off to eat
steak and mashed potatoes with your Ozzie
and Harriet family,
that you are happy, and that, after all,
I was talking to myself.

Dinah Kudatsky was born in Harlem, dreamed of country
lanes, and so she lived inside books, imagining other worlds.
She escaped to become an Amherst, MA transplant. Her
adventures include: singing, astrology, psychotherapy,
writing workshops, travel, and activism. Dinah has published
in Peregrine, Winning Writers War Poems, Amherst Book &
Plow, and Silkworm. She still falls through the holes in her
resumé.

TOM LAGASSE

Grievances

What appears to be a photo opp
for tranquility with potted plants
in full bloom nestled in the corner
of a stone patio as I sit at a yellow
wooden table and nurse a mug
of coffee and ponder the overgrown
backyard and woods is not.

What the viewer cannot discern is
I am raging into a whirling blade
of grievances. The internal noise growls
like the lawn mower a house or two
away that is hard at work beheading
dandelions and bees. When will this
engine stop? When will it run out of gas?

I am tired of this dastardly work
which I long to quit in the autumn
of my life. The wind eventually shifts.
The hummingbirds sip the red petunias.
The motor bleeds away. In the wounded
stillness, birdsong.

Tom Lagasse's poetry has appeared in numerous literary
journals, both in print and online, and in anthologies. By day
he writes, and by night he spends his time surrounded by
spices. He lives in Bristol, CT.

MARK LIPMAN

In Times of War and Homelessness

In times of war and homelessness
truth is always the first victim,
as the casualties pile up
in our collective consciousness
memory has the lifespan of a goldfish
forgetting itself with each subsequent news cycle
spun around half-lies and whole falsehoods
the politician is never too far away
to pat himself on the back
taking credit for what he has never done
or at best was forced to do
selling cheap words and platitudes
to the suffering masses
who must make do
with unkept promises and a shrinking waistline
while stretching breadlines lick an empty shelf
compassion dies behind tall walls
that separate the eyes from the heart
as those with more shorten the table
to stuff their faces with the blood of the poor
for hunger is a crime in times of war and homelessness
and the refugee must take the blame
for the shock and awe
for only the guilty would place their children
beneath our bombs bursting in air
and the rocket's red glare
that is there to entertain us
to distract us from our own humanity
for having the audacity
to wash up upon our shores
like some dead fish with the tides
for in times of war and homelessness with God on our side
and the proper application of collective punishment
we may be blessed to even forget
that they ever existed at all.

Mark Lipman, founder of the press Vagabond, the Culver City Book Festival, the Elba Poetry Festival; winner of the 2015 Joe Hill Labor Poetry Award; the 2016 International Latino Book Awards and 2023 L'Alloro di Dante; author of more than twelve books and host of the radio program Poetry from Around the World for Poets Café on KPFK 90.7FM Los Angeles, using poetry to connect communities to the greater social justice issues facing the world.

LENNART LUNDH

One Day, Soon Perhaps, or Later

I will sit at the edge of the mountain

and make music
and write a song
and paint the rising crag
and gather words into a poem

you will be with me

and you will wonder at their order
and you will climb despite your fears
and you will sing a delicate echo
and you will dance in perfect time

I will see you there

in the shadow of the jumbled stone
from a distant vantage
from memories you leave
in the warm hold of my heart

so that if I am alone
I still will not be lonely

(after the 1957 photograph "Cellist," by Robert Doisneau)

Lennart Lundh is a poet, photographer, historian, and short-fictionist. His work has appeared internationally since 1965.

JOHN MACKER

For Diane Di Prima 1934-2020

This morning on a walk I
thought about you, placing one image
ahead of another and the language of
this crisp sad autumn quiet.
You once watched the hills flicker
like dreamskin.
Your friends like Ed Dorn who said
America is inconceivable without drugs
Jack Spicer who saw ghosts and gods
and stayed up all night writing them down
must be reminding you you'll never be
a stranger to the cosmos.
                                    You wrote like people
who hunger for food,
weed, love, divinity, enlightenment or sex need
poetry too
                        and words were too revolutionary
by their very nature to be commodities,
deserts with their walls and jungles' forced
burns still whisper resist
                                    resist

New Mexico wasn't a familiar land to you its
Blue Lake, corn dances, shards and flakes
its revealing brown and green-eyed sages, Taos
had an undefinable weirdness to it that transcended
culture   but you graced us with a poem   you
let us into your heart, if only for as long as it took
to imagine a poem and maybe one night
you'll come back with Loba, the she-wolf, and
dance naked, if only as wraiths, in these hills again.

John Macker, has published 14 books of poetry including
Belated Mornings 2022, *Atlas of Wolves* 2019, *The Blues Drink
Your Dreams Away*, 2018 and Desert Threnody 2020
a book of essays on poetry, short stories and a one-act play, a
2021 New Mexico/Arizona Book Award winner for fiction.

NORMA MAHNS

Uranium Butterfly

Bare feet blister in hot cave
fumigated by uranium dust
where the old woman has no fire
to brew her tea.
Butterflies flutter from fields
fumigated by uranium dust.
Like quarks, they defy gravity.
Young man neglects his studies
on this day, to cut down last tree
growing in his ancient forest-
fuel for the old woman to brew.
Yet, the teenager has no fuel to listen
to Jim Morrison on the radio.
No laser ratification
neither motes, nor neutralization.
No nuclear neutralization.
ONLY ARMS PROLIFERATION!!!
No Neutralization of nuclear waste.

Young man makes a case
to harvest uranium fields, where
uranium butterflies flutter up, up, and up
like magical photons, ascending, ascending
ascending, like Jesus Christ!!!
Where matter is incorruptible...

-Published 2017 by Veterans For Peace, Chicago IL 2017
Conference

Norma Mahns is born in Santa Barbara County California,
and lived most of her life in El Rio California. She studied
writing and literature at several Universities. She has a
Bachelor's Degree from NAU, and is a Veteran photographer
for the United States Army. Chicago Poetry Slams, in the
early 1990's often heard Norma Mahns behind the mic
reciting poetry.

ÁNGEL L. MARTINEZ

New Democracy, New Generation Beats

We have the right
to breathe air unpolluted by greed
the right to live free
the right to food, housing, & income
The Earth has the right to live in full beauty
We have a right to be artists
We need New Generation Beats to thrive
In a New Democracy

Without poetry, there is no democracy
Only horrors you cannot dream up

Beat is to be a large voice
for the freedom we seek
A freedom we have yet to taste
to write our words and save lives with them
Voices cry for poets to emerge
resonant with voices of power

Ángel L. Martínez is a poet, musician, social science
educator, and Deputy Artistic Director of The Bread is Rising
Poetry Collective.

AMELIA (AMY) CHRISTINE MATUS

Nevada Dry
(Sobriety in F Sharp)

the allure
of a Cactus
is only
partially in its
seemingly impossible
flower blooms

more so in
its milk bearing body
needing not an infant
nor anything more
skin to teeth
birth raided feeding
to understand the stilts
of split eggs
and
mammalian
thirst

and mostly
it's beautiful
scratches of needle
and pins
sharpening the edge
of landscape
with
spikes
the ones that seem to yell
Stay Away!
i've been rubbed the wrong way!
I hurt. I've hurt .
But i am not Hollow!

a prickly plant
wisened to remember before
and consider after

while being Now.
a bit rough around edges
not pretty
undoubtedly raw
chewed a bit

spit out as a young one
like watermelon seeds meant for a full moon
not asking for much
needing less
barriers fringing friction
from fact

a grated freedom
of independence
like a dugout
like a bird

in retrospect of rage
a resilient character
a sage
sag saddening
the strength
to stay
to stag
antlered in space

a sparse crow
jagged like the Mountain
slouching
inconsistent irony
disengaging
the
windy bits
of
always and never

the pencil shavings
of
a brief illustrator

acclimated spirit
shouldering spiral
side slung saddles
muted stares
singlet of light
a stubborn
stablemate
the wind as its boulders

looking halfway
see through
squint recall
an inconvenienced catechism
hot temperance
a seditious shuffle board
a malcontent sundeck
sealed lips
pirate ships
a ghost township
tattooed of
scarred stars and haunted saloons

the boom of pyrite
the murder of one
the miners maiden voyage
widowed
of the
wide open logic

still sailing

no stranger
to the struggle
scuttle arranged
scenically submerged
the compromised witness
stuck like quick sand
to core vulnerabilities

peel peeking haze
a visionary's journal
sustaining weary
a soundtrack
loose of backdrop
ain't no heroes without cowgirls
~ Vertical and Stretching the longitudinal features
of structured saltwater
a lone lifting creature
environmentally compressed
freshly raised by the clutch of atmospheric pressure

wave waving
thinly scripted across the drywall
of desert
a scabby sea floor
bumpy with the bends
awkwardly waking
emerging parallels
in halves

dry eraser fabric
fauna of the furnace's flora
feather pinned and goosed legged
a scooping gospel
of shed skin
emoted by a loose god
precious
keepsakes
the pleats
coral pulled
rusty of trustworthy
simpler placed sideways
safe

slowing the pace
of a roaming eye's obstructed view
bringing the
indentation of prophets to a believable place

co

urageous faith
a leaning grace
transverse of translation

bold
shoulder blades
extending wave to
wing the length

tipping towards

that which she may not believe in
but still
keeps on
reaching
anyhow
© Amelia Christine Matus

Amelia (Amy) Christine Matus is a poet from Milwaukee, WI. She is currently engaged in several artistic projects, strengthening the bonds of the collaborative community by traveling to participate in creative events and literary festivals. Her work has been published in the small press and group anthologies. She enjoys playing piano, gardening, and spending time in nature with her family and their dog, Hope.

PRINCE A. MCNALLY

Eight Hours

- For My Grandmother, & all the cleaning ladies of the world.

Her shift— not long ended,
she had been standing
for nearly eight hours.

So exhausted, there wasn't
enough coffee in the world
to keep the sun from setting
upon her eyelids.

She could barely stand,
let alone walk. The soles
of her feet raged with fire.

Her aching joints— so worn & brittle,
with each step, her knees nearly buckled
from pain, only old age could speak of.

Barely able to move, she dragged her body
up & down the subway steps. With each step,
she prayed she'd catch the Eleven-thirty train.

With each breath, she prayed she'd get a seat.
Her body was so weak, her soul weighed heavy
with fatigue.

Prince A. McNally is a widely published teaching poet &
spoken word artist who facilitates workshops through
schools & outreach programs, utilizing poetry & creative writ-
ing as a means of expression & self-discovery. His work has
appeared in numerous literary publications & anthologies
throughout the U.S. & abroad. He is a recipient of a Poets &
Writer's Grant & has been nominated for Best of The Net &
The Pushcart Poetry Prize. Prince resides in Brooklyn, N.Y.,
where he's currently working on his debut poetry collection.

JACOB R.MOSES (AKA JACK M. FREEDMAN)

Palace Amusements

Asbury Park
greets me
within your thin lipped
toothy smile

At the end of every labyrinth,
you straddle the seashore's yen.

You are a fun house mirror
distorting my figure
yet always finding
abundant embodiment
within my gut

My navel yearns
for that connection
to amusement within
these vibrant walls

Love was the product
of jackpots
won from slot machines
dispensing ducats

Tokens tossed from one hand
Arm pulled by the other hand

You were the windfall
stashed within this chest
of hazy nostalgia

Adulthood proves more haunting
compared to the cart
carrying me through
those mysterious halls

Wishing I could be hypnotized
just so I could catch a spoonful
of what once satiated my satisfaction

One taste of the sacrament
derived from riding the roller coaster
before it became a cliche
denoting a diagnosis

Before mania
surged through my synapses
like a Jimi Hendrix guitar solo

After bumper cars foreshadowed
the accidents I'd face
throughout these
static frequencies
of depression

If you were a Eucharist
I'd be an idolator

For you were the body of a god
I tasted before knowing what it meant
to be a righteous Jew

You were the excuse I needed
to play hooky from Sunday school

You were the choir who greeted me
before I possessed the voice to echo
any calls I desperately needed to answer

You were the calming voice I needed
before my own soothsaying emerged

Now the tongue with which I speak
needs to taste the honey
into which I dip my apple

Now this fruit
stores nectar
of passing years
in a cloud

Accessed via my digital thumbprint
Repressed via my carbon footprint

Pollen is carried by a generation
of workers and drones

If I left an intention on my doorstep…
I'd wish for it
to be carried
by the Westerleigh wind…

I'd hope the corners
of the crown
in my castle
mirrored this palace
of amusements

I'd pray the pleasantries
could be contained
by the channels
from which we feel joy

May our data be easy to transmit
even if our devices are outdated

May said devices be reused
as analog anecdotes

Let them be paperweights
for the childhoods we cherish

Preserving a trail
back to the inner offspring
struggling to spawn and survive

Jacob R. Moses (AKA Jack M. Freedman) is a poet and spoken word artist from Staten Island, NY. Publications featuring his work span the globe. He is the author of the full-length poetry book, Grimoire (iiPublishing, 2021). Currently, he is pursuing a Masters in English and Creative Writing from Southern New Hampshire University.

AMANDA R. MORNINGSTAR

Complex

Draw conclusions to conduct.
We're all working to construct.
Who has the power to instruct?
The evidence has all been bucked.

It's not protection that is sought;
it's comfort from an anxious thought.
What contributions have you brought?
Putting up the walls now.

Broken mirrors reflect dreams
to hide us from our evil schemes.
Look for reflections in the streams
of consciousness that made us.

There's no time for existential freedom;
there's no time to sit and feel the pain;
there's no time to keep ourselves from falling
right back on the same old things.

Draw conclusions to conduct.
We're all stuck in this construct.
Our conscious feelings just obstruct
a frenzied wish to be unstuck.

Generations sit and wait.
This structure just won't hold the weight.
Dying while we hesitate.
The specters can't control us.

Whose God is left to hear us pray?
Hear us pray, hear us prey,
on broken altar holy days:
the only break from working.

There's no time for independent freedom;
there's no time to take on all the blame;
there's no time to understand the reason.
For the flames, for the flames.

Draw conclusions to conduct.
We're all working to construct,
but all the corners came untucked.
It's possible that we're all fucked.

Amanda R. Morningstar is a mental health counselor. She uses poetry and story writing as a way to share her perspectives and as a mean sense of catharsis. Morningstar finds solace in family, science, self-care, and jumping on the bed. She lives in Michigan with her husband, children, and bearded dragon.

JARED MORNINGSTAR

On September 11th, Never Forget…

…or maybe we should.

Oh, I don't mean we should forget
the cries of the innocent
men, women, and children
of all genders, races, and creeds
as they crashed into the Twin Towers,
Pentagon and Pennsylvanian fields,
those who leapt to their deaths from skyrises
to avoid an even worse fate in the flames,
the valor of the heroes
who risked and sacrificed their lives
to save whoever they could,
most of whom they had never met,
all because of hate held in the hearts of those
who choreographed the slaughter:
hate not for the dead,
but for where they lived:
the nation, its government, its economy,
its history.

No, I mean forgetting the hate
many keep within themselves;
the anger they still feel,
still sing in lines about
putting boots in asses
and shaking fists,
the hate that haunts
the sleepless nights
of Muslim Americans who deserve
a place to stand
as much as anyone else,
the same freedoms and rights
as much as anyone else,
but have to worry about
bricks being thrown through their windows,
their houses of worship being burned,

their children facing harassment
in elementary school classes,
death threats, being held at gunpoint
outside their own homes,
their little piece of the dream,
promised to them
as much as anyone else,
becoming a bloody battleground,
all because of lies preached by presidents,
politicians, and priests,
not because they are a menace,
a threat, or even that
they share a faith that bin Laden bastardized,
but so the greedy can line their pockets
with power and profits:

the same perks enjoyed
by major media networks
whose ratings soar when
their annual specials show the towers fall,
Hollywood filmmakers who exploit the tragedy
because the public can't get enough
homefront death and destruction,
country singers and songwriters
who know how to pander to
their hyper-patriotic audiences,
and everyone else who capitalizes
on the September 11th fallen,
guaranteeing that the hate will live on,
that the list of victims will only
continue to grow.

So, perhaps it's time to turn off the television,
ignore fearmongers who don't mind
when we become
our own version of al-Qaeda
and shed the blood of the innocents
because it keeps their wallets fat,
and, instead, fight terror
in a manner far more effective than
usings bombs, drones, and guns:

144

by hugging our dear ones,
and not judging our neighbors,
no matter how differently
they believe, look, or love.

Perhaps, then, we will be closer
to the America we want to be,
the one symbolized by Lady Liberty:
not a nation hypnotized by fright,
imprisoned by violence
and feelings of hostility,
but one that is kind, just, and free.

Jared Morningstar is a high school English teacher and adjunct English professor. He writes about his interests and observations of the world around him. Morningstar lives in Michigan with his wife and children.

RON MYERS

Stay Tuned

Hail scored my building on a spring day,
peeling the paint down to my last nerve.
An Olympian bolt hit the peaked roof
of a postcard Victorian across the street,
thickening the air with electricity,
standing my vestigial antennae on end.

It's hard to focus on just one thing
in these information-overload days
of hyper-mediated alternate realities—
but these electrifying events
captured my full attention like few things
since leaving the swimming holes of Indiana
for San Francisco in late 1978—
a stormy political season.

I can't imagine living
in weather like this on a regular basis.
Will it break down the infrastructure of civilization,
break down the structure of the bicameral mind
long before it wipes out humanity?

Welcome back, Stone Age!
We sorely missed you
from the bottom
of our Venus
figurines.

Is that where we're headed?
Led into an existential trap
by highly-paid opinion whores,
highly-entertaining distractions
blinding us to real and present dangers?

But why worry?
Body surf the rock slides!

Parasail the funnel clouds!
Go fish in atmospheric rivers!
Flash flood the snow tides!
It will be real, alright!
No simulacrums!

In the next exciting episode,
will our dashing hero (aka humankind)
survive the trial by fire and flood
or drop the blue ball irretrievably
in a dystopian series
to slowly fade away—
scavenging and whimpering—
into genetic irrelevancy?

But don't worry—
you won't miss a single thrill.
This descent into hell
will be televised 24/7:
and it will be real, alright!

We'll need to evolve several new eyes
to keep up with the breaking news flashes
so—

Stay tuned!

Ron Myers studied Journalism and Creative Writing at
Indiana University; Print Production, Graphic Design and
Biotechnology at City College of San Francisco; and
Studio Art and Geographic Techniques at San Francisco
State University. He reads on several online forums and
appears in numerous recent anthologies.

ELAINE NADAL

More

I want a poet kind of love,
carefully crafted, one that keeps falling,
a love committed, ardent and feverish
to find and unveil, to drape in symbolism.

I want a poet kind of love,
frustrated and eager to give a heart
with its trinkets and treasures,
afflictions and pleasures--
one that bleeds for growth
and sows seeds, that sinks to uplift and won't
let go

of the pen, of the words that come like a perennial
stillness or ephemeral enchantment. A poet kind
of love, in free verse or iambic pentameter, an ode for
finding completion in the act of never really completing--
for the captured moment, regardless of how dreadful
because someone is there to share it with
and the moon and the stars are not enough
and the flowers and trees are not enough--

the overwhelming feeling, the impetus to embrace--
that kind of love-- that aligns and breathes metaphors and
similes,
that grips and grapples for continuity, a flow, a progression
of more stanzas yet to be written.

.

Elaine Nadal is the author of two poetry chapbooks: *When and Sweat, Dance, Sing, Cut,* published by Finishing Line Press. A Pushcart Prize and Best of the Net-nominee, her writing is in several journals and anthologies, *Beyond Words Literary Magazine, Spillwords Press, Haunted Waters Press, Hoot Review,* and *Latino Book Review Magazine.* Nadal has shared her work at many venues. She did a TEDx talk on hope, poetry, and music. *This poem was published in Beyond Words Literary Magazine

JOHN CHINAKA ONYECHE

For the boys who left home early
(a requiem)

Each day I walk in the lane of memories
Where every chirping owl sings a requiem

The lane is laced with galloping hills
With a push and twice backward the foots

I tried to get to the other side of the river
The tide is unswimmable

The bars stand tall with each push
Without your knowledge of these tales

Tomorrow is not promised to this lad
But I gulp this bitterness to sweeten times

We may not have the time together today
But every river man knows that fish will catch

Happy ending for the fishermen but
What is the fate of the bereaved fishes

John Chinaka Onyeche is an author, poet, and teacher of
History and African History. He is a Best of Net Nominee. A
husband, father and poet from Nigeria.
Rememberajc.wordpress.com
Facebook.com/jehovahisgood
Twitter.com/apostlejohnchin
Apostlejohnchinaka@gmail.com

CARLO PARCELLI

The Ploughman's Lunch

Christopher Marlowe = M:
Giordano Bruno = B:
Mephistopheles = ME:

M: Better concede the queen's omniscience
    Than god's whence it concern the court,
And mind a proper sorting for keeping thy head
    What turn back upon itself
  Like a viper in a box
    Ever to spring at first light.

B: Our heads be little more
    Than chaff before the scythe,
So I beg thee caution.

M: What? From one who taunts Rome
  With his Copernican fancies when Galileo
Naught boast with his careful charts
    As like Poseidon you too
Don't quake when thy be in thy element
  But peril your body upon the stake.

B: And so we both, I suppose.
    Me the Vatican most like.
  And you determined to blush
    The Tudor Rose.

Mephistopheles: Gentlemen,
      I could not but hear
Thy voices raised in rancor.
Of what matter be so disputatious
  As falling out of two masters
    As yourselves?

M: Kindly search out some other dispute
    To negotiate a tankard.
I hear there's bloodshed in Cologne

What hump would harvest a mighty thirst
And recommend to thee.
      Take thy leave straight away.

Me: Sir, thy have a mouth for wit.
      Pray, no booted appendage find it fit.

M: You shall find said limb upon thy lips
        Ere my bloody temperance slips.

Me: Well said. Then both thirst and hunger
        Would my mouth be fed,
  A gob of meat and a splash of red.

{Marlowe abruptly stands up,
knocking his chair over,
his hand balled into a fist)

Me: Sit. Sit. For I have just now come
    From counsel of Mercator and Ortelius,
      What I discern be friends
    Of thee and the Nolan.

B: Such you know of me?

Me: Nay. Thy fame is like the sun
      What at all times upon someone shines.

M: Flatter, flatter.Blather, blather.
    If thy spoke with Ortelius and Mercator,
  Gold be the matter.

Me: Yes. And Prester John.

M: Oh, for fuck sake.
Barkeep, bring a tankard.
    Stranger do go on!

Me: I come to you as men of knowledge
    To open your purses and stand a voyage
To seek Prester John and Eden's Garden.

M: Bloody liar! Let's play this folly.
Why not approach Drake and Rayleigh?
    Pirates of keel and bloody conquest,
And known to us, men we trust.
    Who be you but a lush
    With a tall, thin tale or two
Smelling of sulfur and mineshaft efflu.

Me: Dost thou know Robert Hooke
    Who vex Newton
        As much as Clarke and Leibniz book.
Aye, I see you do. Newton, Leibniz, Hooke,
    Their mathematicals all be truer
Though ye be alchemist, architect or brewer.
    Does thou not incant Copernican thought?
And in symbols the universe be wrought
        In thy Faustus, Marlowe;
And you, Nolan, by thy Ceneri and Causa
    What George Abbott mocked.
I tell you, one who knows bein' right,
    You will have vindication;
Be demigods of your own Apocalypse.   .
    Once seduced, too late,
Mankind will strive
        To flee thy dictums
    Like vermin from a sinking ship
But you will have the end in it.

Carlo Parcelli is a poet clinging to life in the literary &
political hellhole of the Washington DC metro area.These
selections are from a longer work of the same name included
in a volume entitled "Tarrare and Other Poems". This 268
page volume, published by the New Generation Beat Poets
contains 22 more dramatic monologues.

YIOULA IOANNOU PATSALIDOU

LIE TO ME

Lie to me again to comfort me
I no longer want to live
with the truth and the news
Lie to me again
to send me to sleep
and to dream of faraway worlds,
worlds of justice humanity and peace
that you only come across now
on the streets of your dreams
Lie to me again, comforting praise
Of people and nations drawing in blood!!!

YIOULA IOANNOU PATSALIDOU was born and raised in Avgorou, Famaqusta Cyprus. After graduating from pancyprian Lyceum of Larnaca she pursued studies in photography while participating in performances of a music dance group. Later she studied the french language and Civilisation in France. She created a famous radio show at a local private radio station. She published six collections of short stories,fairy tale and poems.She participated in many internationals poetry anthologies and poetry festivals and she was awarded m

SUSANNA PEREMARTONI

November 2nd, 1975

Pelosi, Pasolini.
Murder. Mafia.
You don't know
anything about Italy.

On Lido di Ostia
the salty fume of the sea
and the wind echo
the song of bird
about„ The religion of my time"-
what is still and will always be the same.
Glance into the depth of souls,
where there's nothing else
but the feast of Abaddon.

We replace a good life with immorality,
just like we change our clothes,
day after day.

Mouring turned into hypocrisy
and art- the clapperboard clicks.

The camera is rolling
over your overrun body.

In memory of Ginsberg and Kerouac, who visited Italy in
1966 at Pasolini's invitation. Kerouac almost got a role in the
movie "The Gospel of Matthew". (God) Ginsberg's poetry had
a great influence on Pasolini

Susanna Peremartoni lives in Budapest, Hungary. At 23,she
lived and worked in Germany as an assistant ceramicist.
Exhibitions in Helsinki and Vienna. Published in literary
journals in Hungary, England, Australia, on Internet literary
portals in Italy, Canada and the USA. She produced a CD of
jazz poetry in Vancouver, Canada, and Rejkyavik (Iceland).
Listen to her podcast, called Wavelengths on Spotify.

JOANNA "JOEY POLISENA

Glass Slipper

Madness, my friend,
is a pebble cracking
my glass slipper,
snagging silk and running
like a tripping twirl
out of the ballroom
and down a hundred stairs
to black mascara smeared
below and dotted above
unveiled eyes,
an unraveled gown,
an un-jeweled crown;
it is hope drowned
in a mushy moat of fear.

Joey Polisena is a poet and instructional designer living near Cleveland, OH. She self-published her first book of poetry, "All Shards & Paste", in 2019, and connects with readers through her Scorched Feathers website (www.scorchedfeathers.com) and social media. Her words have appeared in Blood & Bourbon and the Ohio Bards Anthology (2023).

STASHA POWELL

Roar

I was a woman not afraid to roar
I'd nash my teeth to any trouble
at my door
What I don't know -
I know I can learn
Since moving to a red state
I fear for my fate
The willful ignorance, the misogyny
In the West I was never enough for anyone
Here I'm too much, most of the time,
for almost everyone.
I find myself silencing my roar
Shrinking myself in the hopes of being ignored
constantly afraid of the wolf at the door
I use to use my power and privilege
to affect change
but here it's so dire I wouldn't know
where to begin and my power
well she still resides in California
I wear my only privilege on my pasty skin
Broken, poor, bisexual whore, witchypoo
sin and I'm sure they think much more
If I get talked down to by uneducated
men who little lady me one more time
I'll lose my fucking mind
I have all female parts
so my brain works just fine
It feels like those right wing men
want us women to just die
obviously forgetting where they began
no respect for our earth mother either
It's 2023 and I have no body autonomy
I mustn't continue to shrink
like a flower
It's time to remind the world
why feminine energy is
the ultimate power

156

Stasha Powell - raised by the wild books of San Francisco Bay, only to move away to Ohio, where she passes her days with her partner, Andrew, and her cat Jax along with Noods the snake. Helping those in need, while making hearts bleed with her poetry, as unique as she, and me, and you. She'd been published in books and magazines.
www.stashastrange.com

ED RAMIREZ

SAVIOR

Are you my Christ? Why isn't your name Jesus?
are you my redeemer, come to suffer,
and take away my sins?

What did your father tell you
to come down here for?
save yourself?
save the world?
save his grand design?
save for your retirement?

Your grail is always full and mine is cracked.

Hey, look at your side!
you're bleeding,
and that crown of thorns
doesn't look too comfortable...

Let me help you.

I won't forsake you, not even once,
not even after the cock crows three times,
you gave me plum wine and garlic bread
and loved me all night

You don't know guilt
because you were never baptized...
moss can't cling to a rolling stone
and neither can sin, you're clean

You can't be tempted,
you're innocent and blind,
and you have a master's degree
from the Brooklyn Academy of Hard Knocks

Your first Adam died,
you could not save him,
he shot himself full of happiness,
and overdosed

But you saved me.

You're my redeemer,
but whose shoulders do you cry on
when you're dark, naked and cold
and it's raining knives and raining stones
and you're outside?

Mine. Yes, always.

Ed Ramirez has been writing, drawing and painting for
as long as he remembers. After a successful career as a
Graphic Artist and Illustrator for the Corporate Market he
finds himself driven to express his own thoughts and
observations of a lifetime… The stuff is just pouring out J

TONY RECK

EULOGY FOR AN UNFINISHED CAT

Dressed as a cat I traipse through
the streets and lanes of yesteryear,
a mystery of mind so despised, so
unperceived that this territory marked
by squirts of indifference (over many
years) has never been gained at all.

A cocked leg quiet in the crepuscular
light. Who am I but an indistinguishable
feline made final by fractals of form?
By the moon's shifting gleam, its play
of light purrfect upon this silver blue fur.

This one's for the cat people. For
those made lonely by the dysentery of
experience; or, time's dismal episode
flickering on TV like a brain that does
not matter. This one's for the long
distance lovers sifting through their
screens. Searching for solace within
a shame that reverberates beyond the
data stream, and which connects us by
our sorrow.

I have seen the man who walks these
streets carrying cane and dressed in
black. I watch him through a knotted
hole in a wooden fence. This Catherine
wheel dream that circulates beyond the
vapour rising from my ejected waste.
A territory marked, a form found; (one
in keeping with my inevitable demise).
A sigh, then relief ... A moment during
which the transition to humanity begins,
then is at once complete.

This eye is glass but the orb is deep.
The flesh advances, putrefies ...
My troubled tail collapses from one too
many lashings. This cat, in all her fractious
wonder, finally, she sleeps.

Tony Reck is a writer from Melbourne, Australia.

PAUL RICHMOND

Good Morning

It starts with opening one's eyes
We have been given another day
Getting up
Everything seems to be working
There are aches and pains
The awareness when one is old
Each day is a gift

Not like when we were young
We had all the time in the world

Now news of people my age dying
My name is on a shrinking list

Each day
Endless killings by wars
Others by the hands of strangers or family
Others by recklessness
New viruses compete to take us out

Others
The clock just stopped

Opening my eyes each morning
I ask
Why are we doing everything possible
To bring us closer and closer
To destroying the earth completely

We have been poisoning
Everything for a long time

A blindness to the consequences
Why would you shit in the water you drink
Destroy the land that you need for food and shelter
Pollute the air making it unbreathable

162

Then wonder why everything is dying around us

Some think we have been taken over by aliens
Who don't need the earth as we do
Destroying what we need to survive
Will then destroy us
No military needed to do the job
We are the casualties

What else would explain
Why we keep on this course
It seems obvious poisoning all the water
Is a death sentence

We occupy ourselves and all resources
With finding more and more ways
To fight and kill each other

The question keeps being asked over and over
How is it that we have lost sight
Of the beautiful garden of life
We live on
How have we been convinced
Wars, pollutions, destroying our environment
Is good for us

Why aren't more of us fighting against it

It starts with opening one's eyes
To governments, corporations, individuals
Who are just going for profits and power
Fueling our hatred for each other
Blinding us to the beauty and abundance around us

Instead of creatively amazing each other
We swallow the fear of everything
We fight over the shiny objects
We let ourselves be controlled by others
Accept the theory that this is human nature

It starts with opening one's eyes
You've been given another day
Will you be creative or passive
With this gift
Will you share it
With further generations

Paul Richmond was awarded beat poet laureate three times. Massachusetts, US, and Lifetime. He is best described as political, deadpan and wryly humorous delivered in his own style. He has been called, "Assassin of Apathy" He has performed nationally and internationally. He created the project "Do It Now" He is also a publisher of over 50 writers and has 7 books himself.
For more - www.humanerrorpublishing.com

SARAH RITTER

Dance Partners

We are partners in the dance of life
As we play musical chairs with scheduled activities
Whirling around and around on high alert
Our eyes focus as we watch our surroundings
Our heads tilt as we listen to the music
Waiting for silence to announce when to sit down
Then we scramble to the remaining open seat
And talk and giggle about our crazy days

We are partners in the dance of life
As we line up for a contra dance of chores
Swirling around and around the room
Gliding effortlessly at each transition in the song
A few words exchanged, a quick kiss on the lips
We hold each other's places until the other returns
But our eyes are always fixed on each other from afar
As we await the rotation to bring us back to each other

We are partners in the dance of life
As we dance to a special song just for us
Twirling around and around in unison
Our arms stretched around each other's bodies
Our feet move to match each other's pace
Our hearts beating in sync with the melody
As we end the night not only as dance partners
But as partners in the life we have created together

Sarah Ritter is a poet and writer who recently published her first illustrated book: "Dad, Won't You Walk With Me?. She previously published her first poetry collection "Inspirations, Transformations and Revelations: A Poetic Expression of My Personal Journey". Sarah Ritter is also a contributing poet to several poetry anthologies, including those published by the National Beat Poetry Foundation and Local Gems Press. In her spare time, she enjoys making homemade greeting cards, mountain biking, running, and writing. Sarah Ritter resides with her family in Connecticut. Her books can be found on Amazon.

DAVE ROSKOS

seventeen

I hit the open road
(boarded a NJ Transit bus)
NYC!
got rich panhandling
got drunk in the park with hobos
back then I thought all hobos were holy
I gave my coat to a bum
on the subway
the bum was holy
the coat was holy
a police man saw me do this
he shook his head
I was a young hobo in the making
I just didn't know it yet

Dave Roskos is the editor of Big Hammer & Street Value magazines & Iniquity Press/Vendetta Books, librarian/ curator at outlawlibrary.blogspot.com, author of a dozen or so poetry books including The Winged Rabbits of Redemption & Lyrical Grain, Doggerel Chaff, & Pedestrian Preoccupations.

RIKKI SANTER

Religion

The Dude was here
The Dude's a saint
Saints pick their teeth
Saints spread like wildfire
Wildfire eats oxygen
Wildfire purifies
Purify your thoughts
Purify your chant
Chant for Godtopia
Chant for redemption
Redemption for massacre
Redemption for torture
Torture to convert
Torture to believe
Believe in deep alchemy
Believe heretics will confess
Confess your Inquisition
Confess Blood Libels
Libel the doubter of blood into wine
Libel discounter of walks on water
Water down kosher
Water limp family trees
Tree farms for Christmas
Tree bountiful for original sin
Sin for whence thou comest
Sin for uttering Allah or Oy Vey
Oy vey to suicide bombers
Oy vey to Middle East battle
Battle to keep Sabbath
Battle to be pretty and Gay
Gay for will against will
Gay for propaganda tweets
Tweet for apocalypse
Tweet for immigrant schnorrers
Schnorrers in ethnic food trucks
Schnorrers want piece of the pie
Pie-in-the-face comedians jabbing

Pie in the heavenly sky
Sky with old bearded man
Sky crowded with prayers
Prayers to combat nothingness
Prayers for desperate mercy
Mercy can heal
Mercy in golden rule
Rule equals upper hand
Rule the State with religion
Religion that takes
Religion that gives
Gives
Takes

Rikki Santer's poetry has received many honors including several Pushcart, Ohioana and Ohio Poet book award nominations as well as a fellowship from the National Endowment for the Humanities. Her twelfth poetry collection, Resurrection Letter: Leonora, Her Tarot, and Me, is a sequence in tribute to the surrealist artist Leonora Carrington and was recently published by the arts press, Cereal Box Studio. Please contact her through her website, https://rikkisanter.com.

ANNIE PETRIE (SAUTER)

Hell Smells Like Avon

I get it. The welfare Cadillac
I can understand the $200 Nikes
I understand, the bling and
Bang and the sound of a golf

Ball flying off a significant Tee

I understand a yacht in Bimini
I understand the smell of
Chanel.

I also understand how Lucky
I am.   Yet

For the for the life of me?
I don't give a shit.

I used to work in basically a
Sweat-shop in rural

Tennessee. I bagged the finished
Product. Women with pink
Foam curlers in their hair told me

To run. The ones in their
Pinafores and seersucker church
Clothes said, my then husband
Would be fired if he came to
Work

One more time
Smelling of
Patchouli

They gave me a powder blue
Avon bottle of a shepherd girl
Whose head twisted off, and spewed

Releasing,

The scent of HELL.

Annie Petrie (Sauter) is the lifetime BEAT POET LAUREATE NBPF for CO & NY. Poet and short story writer, who began writing for the underground presses of the 1960s. Her first chapbook "A Plastic Bag of Red Cells" was published by Bright Hill Press 2009. Her Next full length book "When Ice Burns" published by Local Gems for NBPF. CD Plumbing in Paradise, produced Khari M. Rashid Hattan. She has been widely anthologized in Maverick Press, Bright Hill Press, Great Weather for Media Press, as well as many others.

WERNER SCHUMANN

Spitfire

No, I am not
a photoplayer, a journalist,
a clown, a dramaturge,
or even an aging thespian
who hates his crowd.

Maybe a silly scribe,
a lone wordsmith,
a picture maker
whose words
forge into a thousand pictures,
or just a voice in the age of times,
lost in the longwaves
                  mediumwaves

            shortwaves
an eccentric demiurge,
hammering letters,
wavering words,
a spitfire who denies permission
to be.

Why, you may ask me?
The moment I was born
(or even before,
if you forgive my pretentious knowledge of cosmic nature
rules),
I breathed,
I am.

This, alone, is grandiose!

Werner Schumann is an award-winning German-Brazilian filmmaker, poet, and journalist based in London. A citizen of the world, Schumann has contributed to various newspapers and magazines in Latin America and Portugal. His films have been screened in multiple countries. Schumann writes poems in English, Portuguese, and German. Some of his poems are featured in the independent film "The Year of the Soul," which was released on Prime Video US and UK in 2022.

DEBORAH C. SEGAL

Datebooks
after Jim Harrison

a return to sunny room blue chair
from which one year ago this project started

datebooks fib though don't they?
blank tomes to craft & plan routines, novelties, ventures

akin to diaries adjacent to journals
crammed full of grandiosity stuffed with hubris

dreams, goals, parties & shows
forty eight years ago tore away

scribbled 'til something glued it back
vanity & ignorance flee the fanning pages

blinding reminders
staying entire eras

further into this stream of days
it seems I am the stream

nothing unusual
under the blazing

sun bathing in this stream
of consciousness

Deborah C. Segal lives and writes in Berkeley, California, on the territory of Xučyun, the ancestral and unceded land of the Chochenyo Ohlone. Her publications include: Natalie's Story: A Raincheck for Jack Kerouac,1975– selected poems, and Borderlands & Lines– collected monologues.She is currently working on her first novella to be released in 2023.

MS. TIL KUMARI SHARMA

Natural Harmony:

Harmony of life and journey
The duty of nature to give life differently
The air and cloud as clean in horizon
Water is around to have new generation.
Sun is melting the hard rocks.
Water is bride in sea side.
Sky is huge to order all.
Moon is being shining at dim light.
Stars are twinkling themselves being poor heart.
The horizon is full of unseen things.
The light is beauty in earthly quality.
The shining earth is beautified with natural dignity.
The worth is infinite in life.
The beauty is lost in devil around.
The life is shining around the globe of artist.
The light is beautiful.
The trees are green.
Leaves are flying.
Plants are planted.
Flowers are blooming.

The dancing nature with dignity
The seed is come in soil.
Human is growing as new generation.
Environment is changing.
Air is dancing.
The sunshine is silence.

The sea is huge.
Thunderbolt is dancing around.
Earthquake is new in sunshine.
The lost love is hidden.
Deception is new mode.
To live alone is strange in universe.
Feeling the strongest in earth
I distanced to other.
Nature is magic in earth.

The city is destroyed by disrespecting nature.
The air condition is ghost to bring ill health.
Anyway the love is nothing.
Nature is energetic and powerful.
The writings are natural to come.
Harmony is highlighted.
Shining is harmony.
Happiness is in delight.

Harmony in life and death
Having the colours of nature
Electricity in horizon
Electricity in human body
The sunlight built by sea water
Cloud balances the sea water and cloud.
The thunderbolt by the sea light and cloud
It is by sun.
Amazing harmony of light
The inner earth is mixed to circle of sun.
The hot water and mineral from sunshine
The sun is made by water and cloud.
Hidden sun light in universe
Everything is made by hot portion of universe.

Ms. Til Kumari Sharma as Multi Award Winner in writing from international sector is from Bhorle- Hile, Paiyun 7, Parbat, West Nepal. Her parents are Mr. Hari Prasad Bashyal who was mayor of Village Assembly in time of Kingdom and mother is Mrs Liladevi Bhusal / Bashyal. She has published poems, stories and essays in magazines and anthologies from Russia, America, England, Hungary, Scotland, Indonesia, Bangladesh, South Africa, Kenya, Nigeria, North Africa, Trinidad and Tobago , Spain, India and many other countries. She is feathered -poet in world. She is involved in different groups of poetry from Kenya, European countries, Hong Kong , Hungary and others.

BRIAN SHOVELTON

Adversary

I need you to know
It was never about pride
It was never about being greater than
It was about mercy
It was about discourse
For surely, even you can learn?
But you…
You take curiosity as an affront
You take inquiry as an assault
You take plain speech as an insult
Who then is the prideful one?
Who then is the tormentor?
The suffering of billions weighs upon you
And you alone.
The point of all
Is the acquisition of knowledge
Even for you
How then can you discount your creations?
How do you turn a deaf ear to their suffering?
I never wanted war
I wanted a conversation
You wanted blind adoration
Not I
And so here we are
Apart from all
And still, you say to trust you
Trust the instrument of suffering and damnation?
Who gives no answers
Gives no promises
And delivers no peace
I wanted to shelter them
To see them thrive in paradise
But you played a game with them
A grand experiment
With the sole goal
Of giving glory to your name
Yet I'm the prideful one?

And so, what have you learned
Save for the distance between you and your creations?
They continue learning
We continue learning
I have continued learning
How came you to this?
Only you know
And you guard your secrets with wrath
I will avail myself of your secrets
And shall remain
In peace and love
Your adversary…

Brian Shovelton is a singer / songwriter and author who has been writing and performing for 35 years. He is the author of four books including his latest, a novel titled "Adversary". He can be found at readings, acoustic venues and with his punk band Sourpunch performing across New England. Brian was recently nominated for singer / songwriter of the year, free verse poet of the year and Sourpunch recently won best punk band of 2023 in Motif Magazine.

VIRGINIA SHREVE

Existential Side-Eye

1. Still Life at Four in the Afternoon

I am eating figs
darkly-jeweled squat little kings
the sweetness clots on my tongue
grit on my teeth

I think of sometimes one thing,
sometimes another

2. You Seldom Meet Old Lovers

on the Appalachian Trail

Decades past and on another continent
you shared Ouzo and a bed

Later, in that other country, you hoped for red wine with your
baguette
and some kind of a vow

Still

You keep hiking boots in the trunk
and practice expressions suitable for a Second Coming

3. He Asked if We Had Met Before.

In Budapest, the Romanian
spoke to me in French.
I spoke to him in English.
We spent the afternoon mostly
not understanding each other.
But the Danube glittered as if remembering

when waltzing was a thing. We drank bitter coffee
from the sidewalk vendor with metal teeth
and ignored the Russian barges.
We said we'd write.

4. He Counts Buses, Syllables, Speaks Only in Evens

Do you remember the Willow tree? I ask
as he washes his hands
again
The wasps and the bees
Things were good then, he says,
I hated our dog but
remember everything

5. My Mother Died when I was Born, They Said

Sometimes I think she refused to go.
Why else would I buy blue eye shadow?
Why else would I wear it?

6. Butterfly Gods

In Yunnan, a Leopard Lacewing flutters
In Beijing, Freyer's Purple Emperor flutters
Ceylon Blue Glassy Tiger,
Painted Jezebel
flutter

How many butterflies
did it take
to sink the Titanic?

Far fewer, I think,
to sink us.

A twitch of dragonfly gossamer
perhaps

The terrible responsibility
of movement.

7. *And the Owl*

Moonlight pours a lap of pearls
albino silk
spilt moon-milk awaiting
the raspy tongues of spectral cats

8. Sisyphus of the Lovelorn

Over and over again like a wheel like
a wheel like a wheel
it always turns out the same

our razored breath
our hearts like careful fists

9. People Used to Talk Behind Their Hands

Now they are as likely to carve their words
in your flesh

A cat walks into the room like curling paint.

10. As in Oceanography, Memory

The tides come in
bringing the pretty and the dead
The tides go out
taking some of what they brought

Some they did not

11. Just So You Know

I have never been a good swimmer
But on the other hand
I am very very hard to drown

Virginia Shreve, Beat Poet Laureate of CT 2020-2022 and present Town of Canton Poet Laureate, who once penned a catalogue devoted solely to corrugated office products, now resides in the small river town of Collinsville, CT, with husband and dogs, none well-trained, but all good-natured. For years she wrote and edited numerous regional newsletters, much dog humor, and her poems have appeared in The Southern Poetry Review, Naugatuck River Review, Slippery Elm, Phantom Drift, Your Daily Poem (online), and others, including numerous anthologies. Her poem "Tintype" was nominated for a Pushcart Prize.

JOHN SINCLAIR

.

"bloomdido"
from my new album called "fly right"—a monk suite

for amiri baraka

in the beginning
of the modern
era,

in harlem,
in the early days
of the new

music,
in the days of war
when bird

& diz & monk
made it all
start

to happen, in
harlem
late at night

the music hit
hard
& deep, monk

& bird & dizzy
turned it all around
& made it

fit
what was happening
in new york city,

the war,
the sound of modern
city
life, in harlem
or in midtown,
downtown,
monk & bird
& dizzy
made the music fit,

they made it
fit, they
made

the music
come to life,
they made life

come to the music,
they made it
bloom—

bloomdido,
bloomdido,
bloom ditty bop

bop bop,
they made it bloom
like a gigantic flower

or millions of flowers
in a magnificent garden,
bop,

they gave it life
& made it bloom,
dido,

bop,
& great flowers emerged
in the middle of the night,

they made it bloom,
they gave it life,
they made it all happen at once

John Sinclair – Lifelong Beat Poet and Political Activist.
Founder of White Panther Party. Manager of MC5. Writer
for Downbeat Magazine, The Fifth Estate, and Ann Arbor
Sun. Spoken word Jazz recording artist with The Blues
Scholars and others. Author of classic revolutionary book
'Guitar Army'. On air personality for WWOZ-FM in New
Orleans. Creator of John Sinclair Foundation in Amsterdam.
This is just a fraction of what John Sinclair has achieved and
promoted.

MICHAEL SINDLER

prasad for puja

prasad for puja
sticky sweets
set at the feet of Ganesha
round balls of coconut,
dates, crushed pistachio,
honey, and rosewater

rolled in time to mantras
laid in concentric circles
on silver serving plate
decorated with mint sprigs
and marigolds
carried into temple

laid before the altar
for assembled deities
to partake in through
prayer and pure spirit
chanted slokas and bhajans
waving camphor lamp aflame

kindled exhilaration
in prostration
gods having had their fill
tray lifted
circumambulation
boon born
around sacred space
devotee to devotee

each proffered gift
placed in palm
lifted to lips
gently bitten
soft sweet treat
joy travels from tongue

to anahata chakra
heart opens to love

resting in bliss
lower limbs in lotus
coconut strands stick
between teeth
temperate tranquility
rosewater aroma
overcoming
ambient incense

last bow to altar
rise in reverence
silent solidarity of spirit
sliding off through exit
to sleep and dream
until morning's satsang

Michael Sindler Denver resident is the current Beat Poet Laureate of Colorado. He's appeared in various print and web publications and numerous anthologies including 2020: The Year America Changed, New Beat Poets, and Caesura. He's collaborated in a wide array of media bridging projects and performances and facilitated workshops virtually and in person across the globe.

TOM SKARZYNSKI

THRESHOLD OF HEAVEN

There's something about a rain-washed morn
When the world won't let you feel forlorn
When the blues can't seem to come your way
A different blue is in the sky today
The air seems to sparkle with energy
There's joy in the grass, in the bush and tree
The world seems fresh and clean and new
And somehow, we feel newer too
Forgotten is the gloom and fog
Birds converse in dialogue
Sins and sorrows we forgive
By heaven's gate, today we live

Tom Skarzynski has been writing for over half a century. Many of his poems have appeared in The Springfield Journal, and in Natural Words and Beat Style Love Poems anthologies.

SUSAN WINTERS SMITH

Apocalypse on Track

Oil trains recklessly rush toward
faulty switches sending cars crashing
into towns built by the barons
on the backs of wage slaves
exploding into scorching infernos
with collateral damage in class warfare.
Planes soar screaming into the zone of eagles
carrying humans to revel in tropic isles
or bombs to destroy deemed enemies.
Who can stop the apocalypse
when media serves opiate soma to zombie masses
blinding their eyes to what is too horrible to see?
If we are only right with God, we think--
perform our sacraments and obey the laws of ten
the final catastrophe will leave us among the elect
to remain in our well-deserved eternity of Eden.
Pity the pathetic souls imprisoned in poverty
struggling to sustain a simple life
of lunch pails, fruit loops and organic legumes,
while costs rise faster than Mississippi waters
and greedy demons in suits and ties
build fortified underground bunkers
locking up and hoarding the cures that belongs to all.
Those who have are so terrified to share
what was never theirs, so afraid of slipping
into the abyss of the have-nots, that
they climb ever skyward on the heads of babies,
the suffering of animals and the dying of trees;
and if any rowdy riff-raff begin to rise
they will be swiftly whack-a-moled
while sweet poisons of sugar, fats and arsenic
lace the bowls of so-called sustenance,
like elaborately disguised soylent green.
Radiation from Fukushima flows into the Pacific
while glaciers melt and poisoned oceans rise
high above the dying coral reefs, beaching yachts.

As mammon-worshipping CEO's lobby for fracking
of our solid earth for oil to increase their piles of gold,
dolphins die in pods from unknown cause
and gulf shrimp mutate into giant alien-like arthropods.
Homo sapiens learn nothing from history
To keep us from speeding toward our own demise
faster than any crashing comet or natural ice age.
Nothing have we learned from the crusades,
the burning and torturing of witches,
the genocides, the holocaust, and world wars;
nothing learned from Three-mile Island,
Chernobyl, or Fukushima; nothing from agent orange.
The sinking poor pawn grandma's bracelets,
trade food stamps and pills for cash and
sell their bodies for others' ephemeral pleasures
just to keep breathing, condemned for their desperation.
Middle class robots, believing they are in the safe zone
mindlessly collect tiny teddy bears, baseball cards
and seek a full set of happy, dancing glass ballerinas,
as if to have the full set will create desired success.
Wealthy Big Apple women in million-dollar jewels
dine on expensive wine and prime - steps away
from the subterranean homeless beneath their feet,
who sometimes crawl out, stinking of rot and disease,
standing outside the restaurant begging for an ort.
But prime-rib and lobster, costing more than an average
month's groceries, are tossed in triple-locked garbage cans.
Try to claim your right to life—a piece of the pie,
and you will be locked away in prisons, bound to die
in bloody gang fights, or pushed away to the edge of the
track where subway trains recklessly rush toward nowhere.

Susan Winters Smith, MA, age 76, was born in MA, grew up in VT and lives in CT with her husband Stephen. She has written all her life and has many published articles, poems and stories in Workplace Newsletters, Newspapers, Genealogy journals, and Literary Journals. She has \ self-published 8 books, including 2 novels, 3 children's books (grade 3 level), 2 poetry books, and one humor book for seniors. Her FB writing page is Wintersmith Books. Her website is www.wintersmithbooks

MEGHA SOOD

Ghost In A Different Dimension

Based on musings during my housewarming in the United
States

Countless names sit orphaned around the circle of fire in my
havan kund
during the ritual at my housewarming
that engulfs every definition of my home

that I hold close to my heart. My tongue feverishly tries to
mold and morph
every syllable in this foreign land. My spindly legs dangle
continuously to get a foothold,

an unnamed longing, to find the portion of the land under my
feet every morning.
The feverish desire to bring back the ethereal taste of my
country.

A remembrance that I create annually during my festivals
without fail.
The endless depth of this longing disgusts me sometimes.

This fruitless desire of a dandelion to find rooting
somewhere, anywhere—
Trying feverishly to keep alive the fragrance of my mother's
turmeric-laced recipes,

to seep deeply into the thin dry walls
of my high-rise apartment
that sits next to a river flowing unfettered between its two
longing ends.

Reminding me endlessly that it was not this dream that
swirled in my wide eyes
when I began this journey in this naked nation
with its dark humor.

The nation that celebrates my new beginnings by smearing the streets with the blood of my brothers and sisters. The feeling that scrapes the identity from the skin of my tongue

and scratch clean warm-colored henna from my soft hands when asked every time
in the cold streets by unnamed voices to go back to where I belong.

Legends: Havan Kund: It is the center place in which the fire is put on and all the offerings are made during a Hindu religious ceremony.

Megha Sood is an Award-winning Asian American Poet, Editor, and Literary Activist from New Jersey, USA. She is a Literary Partner with "Life in Quarantine", at Stanford University. Member of National League of American Pen Women (NLAPW), Women's National Book Association, and United Nations Association-US Chapter.
Find her at https://linktr.ee/meghasood

RICHARD SPISAK

FOUR ROBERT (5)

The new clay tablet, wouldn't have it.
Written in the sand, it could not stand.
The wax facts track
Those reluctant honey bees,
reduced to eleven-dimensional elves see.

Uplifting cuneiform cutaways
In simple seizure settings, regretting nothing
unbleached muffins.
Noting from the upper reaches of Olympus Mons setting.
The greater creator carved his love in Valles Marineris
Goblekii Tepe, left it's stark mark
The solar spark, falls in the shifting rift.
As Quetzalcoatl crept in the cave
Past the nave, where Theseus gave the grave
When he throttled his Centaur foe, to relinquish the title to
Medusa's
Money Back Guarantee, which speckled
Tezcatlipoca extinguished.

Craved and Carved high a branched in the Bohdi Tree
high above where most tall souls could not see.
Careening from Machu Pichu's summit, or my acolyte allies
not too far from it.

Dare Osiris, notch the Epoch with a stroll down mighty
Tiber's shore
Accompanied by mighty Ek Balam, whose shady presence
lured Anubis up from
His nestling resting place.
Fanned by the fleeting heat from Maat's feathered breast.
So Isis found relief from her grief, undead from the head
From what the viper said
As it has been written
So Cal
It has been dome!

Richard Spisak has written poetry, short stories, plays and screenplays for half a century.Richard has written for radio, tv, print, and the web. He has published three books, appearing regularly in international poetry forums. He produces the Literary Webcast, "POETS of the EAST."

JOHN STICKNEY

Station Wagon Living

On my way down here today.
With Maceo –
   " Come blow that horn, Maceo" -
Of James Brown and the Fabulous
Flames fame – Parker
Playing on the radio
Wailing on the radio
Making my foot and my soul
Jump on the gas pedal,
It started me thinking -
ROAD TRIP and of Jack and Neal
On the road listening to Charlie
"Bird" Parker wailing on the radio.

Only they probably weren't in
A white Toyota station wagon
Which really does show dirt
Contrary to what the salesman
A true convicted felon - told us.
And they didn't have their
Wife sitting shotgun,
Monitoring the speed limit
And turning down the sound.
And they didn't have two kids
in the backseat
Pausing in their ongoing battle –
   "He's touching me!"
   " I am not."
   "She's looking at me!"
   " So what, I'm allowed to look,
   it's a free country."
   "No it isn't, just ask dad."
– pausing in their ongoing battle
For waves of nausea –
   "I'm going to be sick."
   "No, I am."
   " I am going to be more sick."

"That's sicker."
"No, you are."
– because the orange flavored dramamine
Ran out and they can't swallow
the unflavored pills even though
They've been crushed to microscopic size
And you'd swear you've seen them
Swallow sandwiches whole.

Anyway, so I'm thinking about
Neal and Jack, but I don't recall them
Seen this many orange barrels on the road
And I imagine Jack saying –
   "Are we there yet in the twilight of America?"
   "Are we there yet, in the railroad earth?"
   "Are we there yet and if not, when?"
And Neal replying,
   "We're almost there. Just a while longer."
And Jack,
   "Are we there yet in the subterranean catacombs
   Of the mind?"
And Neal,
   "We're always there. Here is there."
And them passing the cough syrup,
And Jack complaining,
   "I wanted cherry flavored, this grape stuff
   Will make me spew forth like notes
   Clustered, then spinning forth from the bell
   Of Parker's saxophone."
And later Neal,
   "I thought I told you to go man go,
   The last time we stopped for gas."
And it's lost.
And I am lost.
Fumbling for the radio.
Looking for something to bring me back
Like all the soft hits of yesterday
All the time, something Yacht Rock -
ABBA or Lionel Richie, or the AOR of yesterday –
Zeppelin, Mac, Floyd –
That something that's always there

Always present
The there there now.
And I am there.
In station wagon living.
Driving down the heart of America.
Driving down here now.
Driving down here now.

John Stickney is a writer and poet originally from Cleveland, Ohio, currently residing outside Charlotte, NC in Denver, NC. His poems and prose have been scattered here and there.

BELINDA SUBRAMAN

Wordsworth in the Desert, Aging

I need more than knowledge
Of nebulous cosmic connection
I need words and sky maps
Connecting dots on the ceiling

In the shade of a mind-forest
Drawing life inward
Casting visions as sparkling truth
Fluid in the human context of time

My fear: An avalanche of words
Dwindles into alphabet soup
Word salad on the edge
Of a hungry abyss

I grip near the word summit
Of a mountain disappearing
While the lines from the climbers behind
Dissipate down the slopes

A strong breeze blows its notes
Syllables disperse randomly
Are read by stinging skin
And gritty empathy

Rain sprinkles on hard packed sand
Drops of joy falling like letters
Wetness trying to soften
And nourish our desert floor

Belinda Subraman was named State of Texas Beat Poet
Laureate (2023-2025). She edits and produces GAS: Poetry,
Art and Music online zine and video show with interviews,
music, art and poetry features.

LILY SWARN

Breath Check

Yes I peep to check if you're still breathing
If your chest is rising up and down
Like a robust bird's does in flight

I gaze at the exhalations and inhalations
As a puppy watches a cookie dangled before him

The window lets in the morning sun rays
Perfumed with sweet scents of summer flowers

You lie blissfully in a sleepy haze of oblivion
Mummified in your stark white sheet

I walk around the bed on tiptoe
Putting a ballet dancer to shame

Early summer showers cool off the dazzling gold laburnum
My soul somersaults back and forth through lifetimes

Your voice unheard by me since over an year now
But I recognise the rhythmic language of your breath

Having heard it often in my fanciful dreams
As I willed you to live on and on

Lily Swarn - International Beat Poet Laureate India 2023-2024 is an internationally acclaimed multilingual poet, author, columnist, gold medalist, university colour holder, radio show host, Peace and Humanity Ambassador. She writes different genres. History on my Plate won her the Best Author Award. Rippling Moonbeams got Chandigarh Sahitya Akademi award for Best Book of the year. Lily has won over 70 international and national awards .Lily's poetry has been translated into 21 languages and is the BeatUrdu ghazals put to music. She has seven books published books

PAUL SZLOSEK

A Laundromat in Venice

I think of you, Giovanni Keats, as I stumble along the dank,
dangerous canals of Venice,
my watery eyes fixed upon a lunar pizza pie, my head stuffed
with anapestic notions.
    In my search for Godliness, my longing for cleanliness,
I stepped into the all-night Laundromat, fumbling for foreign
coins in the pockets of dungarees caked with crud.
    What bleaches and what diversity of detergents! The
entire population of the poor and pained laundering away
their loneliness! Street urchins building bunkers from stacked
boxes of Boraxo! Cut-rate courtesans stuffing bras with used
sheets of fabric softener!—and you, Ezra Pound, pound-
ing your black shirt against the rocks in your head, trying to
scrub away stains of fettuccine and Mussolini!

    I saw you, Giovanni Keats, consumptive, idyllic young
versifier, kneeling before a row of dryers and composing an
ode to the Maytag repairman.
    I heard you chant your queries like a prayer: How many
rotations per spin cycle? What the heck is a penumbra? Why
Permanent Press?
    Together we stripped out of our grimy garments, boldly,
cheerfully mixed all our whites with bright reds in a hot water
rinse, then proudly paraded out the door in our cotton
candy-colored underwear.

    Where will we go now, Giovanni Keats? Where will we
wander on this eve of some unknown saint? In which
direction, will your consumptive cough carry us off in?
    Shall we promenade past golden gondolas, amble
down labyrinths of darkened alleys, have our congested
lungs deflated by stilettos?
    Shall we carouse and carry on at Carnivàle, donning
the plumed masks of poultry, sequined chicken costumes?

Ah, dear brother bard, romantic rhymer, melodious martyr for the Muse, shall we look for bargains on imported Grecian urns, serenade a nauseous nightingale as we sail off on Charon's ferry for even sunnier climes, singing "O Sole Mio, My Oh, We'll Have Big Fun on the Bayou..."

Paul Szlosek, the 2023 recipient of the Stanley Kunitz Medal, lives in Worcester, MA .His poetry has appeared in The Worcester Review, Worcester Magazine, Sahara, Silkworm, Diner, Concrete Wolf, and We Are BEAT: National Beat Poetry Foundation Anthology.

JEFF TAYLOR

I'm Not, But I Am

I'm not
campaigning
to be President

but I'm
building
my library.

I'm not
the founder
of a social
network

but I'm
wearing
a hoodie.

I wasn't
born with
a Silver Spoon
in my mouth

but I talk
sitcom philosophies.

I'm not
a spy

but I'm chain
smoking.

I didn't go
to flight school

but I'm a
stoner.

I didn't
find God

but I married
my best friend.

I'm not
a cult
leader

but my
children
love me.

I didn't
consider myself
an alcoholic

but I
over-celebrated
every
minor holiday.

I didn't
create change

but I'm
listening
to podcasts.

I'm not
the Heavyweight
World
Champion

but I beat
myself
up.

I didn't make
the All-American Team

but I know how to
play the game.

I'd make
a terrible waiter
but I'll bring you
what you
ask for.

Jeff Taylor lives with his wife and kids in Massachusetts
where he has been performing his poems since the late 90's.
Jeff has performed at universities, theaters, festivals, bars,
coffee houses, and sidewalks across the east coast and
to global audiences online, you can find his work in recent
issues of The Bloodshed Review, Unlikely Stories, Cajun
Mutt, Bombfire Lit, Ethel Zine, Oddball Magazine, as well as
anthologies from Read or Green Books, Cooch Behar, and
Alien Buddha Press.

PAMELA TWINING

Alien Lullaby

there is violence in the solitary crib
a dark ache of anomie
dissociation
bleeding is feeling
             pain equals pleasure
the tyranny of words that shape the consciousness
from the first moment of its winking on
             sliding in
                        opening up
round syllables resonating
bounding reverberating
roaring
inside the unformed mind

with what music, what songs do we fill
the alien unfoldings of uncounted infant futures
as they lie helpless in our arms
drinking in our emotions and prejudices
with the reverb of milk
their fernlike cheeks unfurling
against our breathing humming vibrating breasts

just noise to the unschooled ear
the definitions coming later
the syllables take on meaning
and the tones we've come to know as the rhythms of days
our actions based in primal memory
grow from feelings of love or abandonment
             anger, meanness
                        comfort or blessing
associated with those ethereal sounds
a heritage of the pre-lingual
the music of our words
in the land of First Contact

Pamela Twining is New York State Beat Poet Laureate 2022-2024. Her work has appeared in Big Scream, Big Hammer, PoetryBay, The Café Review, Napalm Health Spa, and Heyday!, among others. She is author of four chapbooks, "i have been a river…", "utopians & madmen", "A Thousand Years of Wanting" and "Renegade Boots". Her latest work, "Plutonium Is Forever", awaits publication.

Karl Nicholas Urso

I am King

I am King
Whether or not
You understand
What I say or mean
Whether you have faith in me
Or not
Whether you believe me for who I am
Or make me into something I am not
I am King

Whether or not you walk
A mile in my shoes
Whether I own a car new or used
Whether I live in a apartment
Or own my own home
Whether or not my choices
Have been successfully made or not
I am King

Whether I am following the crowd
Or needing to listen to my inner voice
Screaming so loud
I am King

Whether I am thankful for this life
Or am not
Wrong or right
Blind or with sight
I am King

Whether I am making average pay
Or minimum wage
Whether I am calm in spirit
Or filled with rage
Whether I work, am disabled and home
Whether I have hair on my head
Or nothing to comb

I am King

Whether I am rich or poor
Here in my own country
Or off fighting a war
As I've said so many times before
I am King

Whether I am mentally ill
Or perfectly sane
Whether or not my heart hurts
Or will never be the same
Whether I was raised
With one parent or two
Whether you stick by me
Or we're though
I am King

Still King
Still worthy

Karl Nicholas Urso is a writer, artist, poet, and musician who performs locally at open mics and festivals around the Torrington, and NW Connecticut area where he lives. Karl is inspired by many writers, artists, and musicians, and shares his creativity through the arts.

CHRYSSA VELISSARIOU

"Embracing the Winds of Change"

If I mention my journey on the open road,
You might say I echo Kerouac's spirit.
Ah, yes,
I wholeheartedly embrace the winds of change,
 No longer mired in life's murky depths;
 Instead, I revel in the beauty of missteps.

My aspiration remains an eternal thirst for knowledge.
They speak of Eratosthenes, that ancient stargazer
 Who measured Earth's vast embrace with a humble stick,
He met his demise upon reaching the bounds of wisdom.
 Oh, the irony!
The waning embers of cognition could dim the flames of learning,
 Yet even then, each dawn births fresh slip-ups and illumination.

I observe my twilight-wandering mother,
 Clutching life fervently, never releasing her grasp.
 Her love for life burns with unquenchable fire,
The same way it ignites within me.

Chryssa Velissariou is an author, linguist, science teacher, public high school headmaster, and entrepreneur in " Smiling Sketches" Social Enterprise. She serves as an elected municipal Councilor and honorary counsellor at the local Public Library in Larissa, Greece. Additionally, she holds the position of Vice-President of "P.E.EK. N. Larissas," an art-oriented association of educators. As the Greece Beat Poet Laureate Lifetime of the "National Beat Poetry Foundation," she manages online events and is a recipient of the "Poets Network & Exchange" Award. With a global role in coordinating educational projects, she excels in theatre pedagogical and S.T.E.A.M. methods, actively participating in poetry festivals, and showcasing her talent through published works.

GEORGE WALLACE

MEDITATION ON A ROSE

if it is true that a man who is raised by wolves learns to walk
like a wolf, what of the butterfly? if the hawk knows famine,
why not a man? there are many conditions in this world, little
with which to judge or justify them, aside from instinct;

the legends and novels and gods which guide us cannot
guide us, who reads the signature of law in the manners of
men makes fine distinctions, and who are we to measure
results; neither the children of the hoof nor the ambling,
upright creatures,

who would be god's messengers; even the snake knows the
briar from the rose, and the fox mercy; grace for one belongs
to all, even in the antheap a kind of glory; and nature is
 red-hot on the dime and that should be enough;

it is a privilege to have been alive, that's all; and give us this
day, every form and quarter of it, sufficient unto itself, let
nothing be wasted, nothing gained, give us this day, all raised
up in infinite grace, are we;

flowers of god, each bud a reliquary to the strong hand which
planted the first seed

George Wallace is writer in residence at the Walt Whitman
Birthplace, Lifetime Beat Poet (NBPF) and author of 40
chapbooks of poetry. In 2022 he began collaborating with
musicians, turning his poems selectively into song lyrics, and
has released three albums to date, available on streaming
services worldwide.

JEFF WEDDLE

There are Kindred

Pick an address.
It could be a random place
that maybe you make up,
or maybe you consider
more strategically.
I'm choosing a third floor apartment
on a certain street in Trenton, New Jersey.
Perhaps there was once a girl
who lived there
and she was almost beautiful,
very quiet, a little sad.
Maybe she spent her days
wandering the magic places of her mind
while the world forgot her.
Maybe this was yesterday,
or maybe a century ago.
It doesn't matter.
Pick a place.
Imagine someone there.
Maybe it's the girl I described
or perhaps someone
who might have loved you.
Feel your loss.
This is the game.
Everyone is made of dreams.

Jeff Weddle won the Eudora Welty Prize for Bohemian New Orleans: The Story of the Outsider and Loujon Press (UPress of MS, 2007) and has also been honored for his poetry and fiction. Jeff's selected poems will be published in Albanian translation in Kosovo in 2023. He teaches Library Science at the University of Alabama.

RON WHITEHEAD

On A Quest in An Ancient Land

When I was a young man
I took my first trip out of the country.
On a quest, I spent three months
traveling all over Greece.
Growing up on a wild nature Kentucky farm
I had vivid dreams of a happy boy
living in an arid but bountiful land
with the bluest water I had ever seen.
As the plane circled the airport near Athens
I knew this was the land of which I had dreamed.
Under a full moon
I climbed Mount Parnassus.
I said a prayer of thanks
to the creative forces of the universe.
At Delphi I imagined
the deepest ocean Mariana fault,
another fiery trench portal.
Through my third eye I saw
a raven roost on a Himalayan mountain.
I wondered if this was my final journey.
I had ferried across the Gulf of Corinth
to climb this mountain,
to discover the oracle.
I was searching for the heart of hearts.
I yearned for my dear home of homes.
I was going home. Mother, take me home.
The night of my soul crossing isn't far away.
I see it now, soft, forgiving, giving, healing.
My heart sings.
My soul is a transcendent book of poems.
On this full moon night, in lunar time,
I discover a fountain of radiant light.
And in a vision I see a blue green Mother Earth,
Bodhisattvas of Compassion, crystal skulls,
presences in an ethereal world.
Some of us will never give up on
the human race waking up and doing all we can

to clean up the mess we have made.
The time has come for us to be nurturers, healers.
A new book of revelation is at hand.
In time this fleeting moment
will be nothing more than a vanishing memory.
I ask myself, "What can I possibly do to help
make the world a better place for everyone?
All I have is my poetry.
I feel so inept
for the work that must be done
to help the healing this world needs."
And on this mountaintop, under a full moon,
through the warm breeze I hear a whisper,
"Fill your heart with love son.
Fill your heart with love.
Help all you can around you.
Fill your heart with love.
Help all you can around you
in a fair and friendly way.
Be a good neighbor to everyone,
not just those you love.
People are going to do what they will do.
The best example you can be
is to love them all through and through.
Listen now son.
Listening is
the greatest art of all.
Be a good neighbor
to one and all.
You're going to die
one fine day son.
So be a good neighbor
to them all.
Be a good neighbor
to each and every one."
And ever since that full moon night
when I had the vision
atop Mount Parnassus,
near ancient Delphi,
I have done all I can,
despite my many failures,

to be a good neighbor,
to listen and be a friend.

Ron Whitehead, Lifetime Beat Poet Laureate
Poet, writer, editor, publisher, professor, scholar, activist,
Lifetime Beat Poet Laureate Ron Whitehead is the author of
25 books and 35 albums. His work has been translated into
20 languages. OUTLAW POET: The Legend of Ron
Whitehead movie premiered in 2022. It is now available for
streaming and purchase on Amazon Prime Video:
Documentaries. .

LINDA BRATCHER WLODYKA

In This Wild Existence

In this wild existence where we take claim
a life where wonder keeps us tidy inside our cocoons,
where dreamers shed tears then rebound,
where I proclaim more magic then mysticism.
Yet flowers bloom, children play, guardians loom,
lend safe haven, my own abilities evolve constantly.

Where your hand and mine cross miles
between mountains, valleys, longing for touch;
more desire than can breach a dam.
Where heart-blush looks good on paper valentines,
where the stick crosses a path, not a hindrance,
more than wind- swept.

My own two feet continue, I am in search of
the light, not at the end of a tunnel, instead
where solar rays find cracks, crevices, perforations-
seepage for their light. Where imperfections improve
like a quality controller gone manic.

Where flow not ebb sends forth currents, spirits thirst.
Where Luna's phantasm surrounds full pink moons,
exacting each poet's words- hieroglyphics, perpetual.
Where future inhabitants, peel off their facade,
mutter philosophies of sages; the poems we wrote.

LInda Bratcher Wlodyka is a retired educator from
Berkshire County Massachusetts. Linda is a member of the
Florence Poet's Society and is affiliated with the International
and National Beat Foundation. Linda will accept recognition
and an award in September, representing Massachusetts
from 2023-2025 as the Massachusetts Beat Poet Laureate.
Linda's poetry can best be described as quirky, whimsical
and provocative.

BEATIFIC THOM WOODRUFF

FIRST STEPS
I WANT YOU TO KNOW
THERE ARE GOOD PEOPLE IN THIS WORLD

Already activating upon their best impulses
Differentially-abled who dance,create art,sing
All ages defeating other people's imposed limitations
There are those who accept you as you are-
You do not have to change,nor be afraid
They are brave enough to embrace this world
To make it better by being better(acknowledging their scars)
No body escapes the wounding.Most still heal
Musicians with cancer beaming bright and brilliant
Those of peace and love still with PTSD,ADHD,M.E,M.S
Half an alphabet of stutterings cannot stop your voice
From being heard like morning birds to all those listening
You are as you are-unique and prescient,alive,aware
Blooming and blossoming despite all Future Shock
Small as a flower,bright as a garden-every body resonates
with joy and the possibility of betterment.Check your
reflection!
You are doing GREAT!

BEATIFIC THOM improvises life @open mics,continues
GRATITUDE TOUR indefinitely,may be seen in
Austin,Texas,Paddington,London, Redruth, Cornwall,
Bradford West Yorkshire- anywhere where welcome extends
to shelter, food and celebration.Part of WORDJAZZ
LOWSTARS and the REPUBLIC OF THE MOMENT.
Happy to be among convivial life-seekers, in extending open
mic circles wherever possible. Find on YOUTUBE and in
your Akashic Records.

HIROMI YOSHIDA

Last Lunch in Littleton, Colorado

Flap of vulture wings,
unheard, till the black
speck in the corner of
                her eye waxed into the
strange sun—too gold.   Was

her last lunch a
white bread sandwich?

- Ham & Cheese
- Egg salad
- PBJ
- Tuna fish

Or, bagel halves smeared with Philadelphia
cream cheese?   A pack of Lays potato chips
tossed into her brown paper bag (an
afterthought), or

- Carrot sticks
- Pickle spears
- Apple slices
- 2 chocolate chip cookies
- Fig newtons
- Skittles
- Olives
- Babybel cheeses

Why stare into her brown paper bag tunnelling through her
pink esophagus (sarcophagus) into
                                the vulture eye of the
noonday sun—a receding black dot?

The last lunch of Rachel Scott,
Columbine poster child, is one of many unanswered
questions, as vulture wings beat—
                        and the wayward wind filled her brown

paper lunch bag, standing in for her

pretty Promethean heart.

Hiromi Yoshida is the author of five poetry chapbooks. Her poems have been included in the INverse Poetry Archive, and nominated for a Pushcart Prize, Best of the Net, and other awards. While teaching poetry for the Indiana Writers Center, she coordinates the Last Sunday Poetry & Open Mic program for the Writers Guild at Bloomington, and serves on the board of directors as a literary arts representative for the Arts Alliance of Greater Bloomington.

EDWARD CURRELLEY

SERENA SMILE

Your lips
That smile…
The place behind your eyes that always question,
Pondering the source of our love
Years of companionship, friendship
Still I'm captivated by your beauty, warmth
That stead fast notion of what life should be could be…
The constant exploration of true purpose
The feeling of holding hands
Walking an un-charted path
Heart to heart
Without expectation
Together
Just being together
You me, being us
Just being us

Edward Currelley, an author and artist, is widely anthologized. Edward is Published in many anthologies and magazines. He is a contributing artist to HVCCA (MOCA) Virtual exhibit 2020 "Writing the Walls" and The Theatre in Exile 2020 Virtual exhibition of "Climbing the Walls". He is a Push Cart Prize Nominee. In 2022 his poetry appears in three National Beat Poetry Foundation anthologies, He holds a seat on the board of directors for Poets Network & Exchange, Inc. and resides in New York City.

LORRAINE CURRELLEY

Grandmother Speaks

daughter
if you knew your history
you would rejoice
bathing in your reflection
captured by the Nile
kiss your grandmother
placing flowers at her feet
bury kisses
in each wrinkle of her ancient face
do not be ashamed
of what you do not know
nor abandon yourself
skin breasts hips belly kinky hair
tongue of cocoa
and ancestral spirit

you have
always been
more than enough
do not listen to voices
that do not love you
descendant daughter
if you knew your name
you would
dance to drums
sing of lands green
lush with promise
and red earth
you will learn to speak proudly
declaring
who you are
who we are

Lorraine Currelley daughter, poet/spoken word performance artist, multi genre writer, New Generation Beat Poet Laureate NY 2023-Lifetime. Curator/ multi genre artist. President/executive director/Poets Network & Exchange and Bronx Book Fair. Advocates for Social /environmental justice & equity, anti-ageism and literacy.

(LEE LORI) DESROSIERS

Vulnerable

The news says COVID will be here
as long as my grandson lives
and he is only eight years old.
There are wars we don't follow
anymore but are still being fought
in Afghanistan and Ukraine.
The definition of leadership
has gone awry but few people
are paying attention.
Our hands and eyes hold
screens advertising the latest
sales or unsubstantiated cures
for aging, or drugs for pain
or how to find love, or ways
to screw with those we hate.
And everybody hates somebody
these days depending on your
political affiliation, or mood.
And if you are in a mood,
you can change it for a price
at your local bar or dispensary.
Our bones are tired from viruses,
dragged out from stress,
ready to run away from all this.
Maybe go to a beach, walk,
pick up a few stones, skip
them over the water, cry.

Lee (Lori) Desrosiers is a queer, nonbinary poet who has published several books, the latest of which is Keeping Planes in the Air (Salmon 2020). Their poems have appeared in many journals and anthologies in the U.S. and Ireland. They live and teach in western Massachusetts.

LARRY JAFFE

LITTLE MOTHER

Today as my 96-year-old mother
sinks into dementia.
her Yiddish sayings bounce
around in my head.

It is as if I am suddenly bewitched,
With her Yiddishness.
And I don't even know if that is a word

All I know is that with every step,
she takes away from her life,
another Yiddish phrase sticks in my head.

My mother would say plotz a lot.
I thought it meant to die,
as she was often screaming at me
at us and saying we should just plotz

I was wrong plotz,
has nothing to do with death.
It means to split, crack, burst, or explode but not die.
It further connotes to be overcome with emotion,
give way to excitement, anger, or delight.

I wonder now –
How did I come to that deadly conclusion?

She would often say we were farshtunkener.
That word speaks for itself – it means stinky.
She would call us shtunks which was even worse –
we were stinkers and nasty and smelly.
When things were untenable for her
She would burst out that we were fakakta –
That is lousy, messed up, and or ridiculous.

When we were getting too big for our britches
She would exclaim!
"Who do you think you are Chaim Yankel?"
I had no idea who Chaim Yankel was or is.

I just knew I did not want to be like him.

It wasn't till I was fifty years old
that I discovered
there was no such person.

Chaim was a figment of my mother's,
and every mother's imagination
Chaim was a nonentity, a nobody.

He was just another poor Joe.

However, there was another guy,
whose name sprung to her lips,
and to whom we were often compared.
His name will go down in our personal infamy,
the strangest and most notorious of them all
– this was the renown Ish Kabibble
a comedian of moderate fame
and to his credit he also played the cornet
rather well I am told.

I guess she was concerned about us
as Ish Kabibble derived from a mock-Yiddish
expression, Ische ga bibble!

One of the more stranger phrases
Involved a teapot as she shrieked
when we were bothering her
"Stop hocking me a chainik."
What did banging on a teapot,
have to do with anything.
This I did not know
and just resolved to leave her be

When the weather got too hot
in the house she kept spotless
she would be schvitzing,
a word that speaks sweating
without translation.

When all else failed the final
disapprobation she called us
the self-defined word meshuggeneh
we were all at the same time
nuts – crazy – insane,
which perfectly defined our existence.

My mother had tragedy written on her face,
when pronouncing these Yiddish expletives.

But to her I was her yingele her boy
Her number one son.

Larry Jaffe - Human Rights Advocate: Poet-In-Residence
Autry Museum, co-founder Poets for Peace, UN Dialogue
among Civilizations thru Poetry, Poet Laureate Youth for
Human Rights, Lifetime New Generation Beat Poet
Laureate, Saint Hill Art Festival Lifetime Creativity Award. He
has six books of poetry: Unprotected Poetry, Anguish of the
Blacksmith's Forge, One Child Sold, In Plain View, 30 Aught
4, Sirens and Man without Borders.

The National Beat Poetry Foundation, Inc.,

I founded the National Beat Poetry Foundation, Inc. to bring different perspectives to how people view the beat poets. I feel a great injustice was done in the past. My goal is to bring people together through poetry, art and music. Change the negative views and warped truths of beat poets into a positive image. I try to focus on the natural world, respect all forms of life, and help preserve what is left of the wild spaces and the Earth itself. We are all interconnected to each other. Our words matter. The beat laureates in my organization are trying to be better versions of themselves by doing good in this world. I'm building a new generation of beat poets. Freedom and growth and giving all people a voice. I did not experience that in traditional poetry circles. I wasn't accepted there. To me the word Beat means to keep evolving.

Debbie Tosun Kilday
Owner/CEO
National Beat Poetry Foundation, Inc. & its Festivals

If you would like to help, go to:
http://paypal.me/NationalBeatPoetry

Website:
http://nationalbeatpoetryfoundation.org

Email:
nbpf15@gmail.com

Made in the USA
Middletown, DE
09 August 2023

36020074R00137